Getting the Most Out of
RootsMagic

Third Edition

Bruce Buzbee

RootsMagic, Inc.
PO Box 495
Springville, Utah 84663
USA

Trademarks

RootsMagic, SmartMerge, and SmartShare are trademarks of RootsMagic, Inc.

Windows is a registered trademark of Microsoft Corp.

All other brand and product names are trademarks or registered trademarks of their respective companies.

About the Author

Bruce Buzbee is the founder and president of RootsMagic, Inc., and the author of the RootsMagic genealogy software. He has been writing genealogy software for over 15 years.

He is also the webmaster of Family-Reunion.com, a free website designed to help visitors plan the perfect family reunion, as well as the author of Family Reunion Organizer software.

Acknowledgements

To my children Alan, Kristy, Michael, Eric, and Tricia, who think it's cool to have their photo in a book. And to my wife Laurie, who doesn't.

And to my beta testers who not only helped exterminate bugs, but whose advice helped make RootsMagic a better program than I could have created by myself.

Conventions

☺ **Tip**   Advice on easier ways to accomplish a task.

💣 **Warning**   Warns you about things you might not want to do.

✏ **Note**   Additional information about the current topic.

"File, New"   Select these items from the main menu. For example, **"File, New"** means to select **"File"** from the main menu, then select **"New"** from the **"File"** menu.

Ctrl+Tab   A key sequence where the first key (in this case **Ctrl**) is held down while the next key (in this case **Tab**) is pressed and released.

Table of Contents

Introduction

What is RootsMagic?

RootsMagic is a genealogy database program, meaning that its main function is to provide a place to enter information about your family. But while RootsMagic is an easy program to learn to use, it is also one of the most powerful genealogy programs on the market.

Unfortunately, many people will barely touch the tip of the iceberg of RootsMagic's features. Hopefully this book will help you get the most out of your copy of RootsMagic.

How This Book is Organized

This book is not intended to be a software manual. I have tried to make it as informative as possible, while lacing it with insights about how to get the most out of the program.

In the first chapter we will create a sample database with a few individuals to get you up and running using RootsMagic. Subsequent chapters go into detail on various aspects of RootsMagic and your family history. A Quick Summary at the end of the book provides a brief summary of the RootsMagic menu commands, toolbar buttons, and other information.

And finally, while this book will cover RootsMagic from the ground up, it assumes that you have a working knowledge of Windows, such as how to start a program, how menus work, what a dialog box is, etc.

Getting Started

The beginning is the most important part of the work. - Plato

RootsMagic is a very easy program to learn, so we can just jump in and start entering your family. We will be skipping over some details, but don't worry, we will cover them all in later chapters.

Creating a Database

The very first time you run RootsMagic you will see a "Tip of the Day". You can view tips about how to use RootsMagic, and when you are ready to continue, just click the "Close" button. You will then see a blank screen that looks like this:

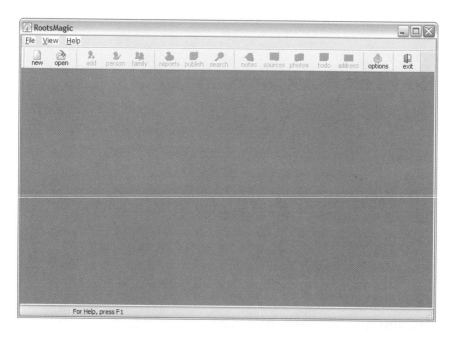

The first thing we will do is create a new database. There are two ways to do this; select "File, New" from the main menu, or click the "New" button on the toolbar (it looks like the button at the start of this paragraph). RootsMagic will ask you to enter a name for the new database. Enter the filename you want, click the "Save" (or "OK") button, and the following dialog box will appear.

Simply select the options you want. Don't worry if you aren't sure which settings you want to use. You can always change them later. After you have made your choices, simply click the OK button, and you have just created a new database to hold your information.

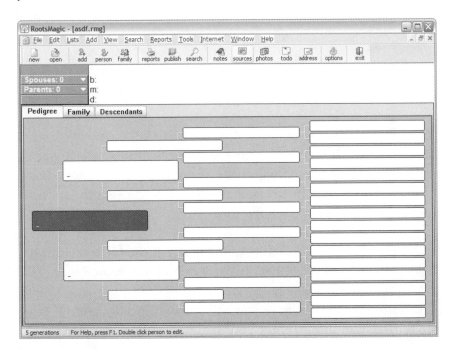

The main RootsMagic screen looks like a five generation family tree. As you add people to your database, RootsMagic adds their names to the tree.

Adding Yourself

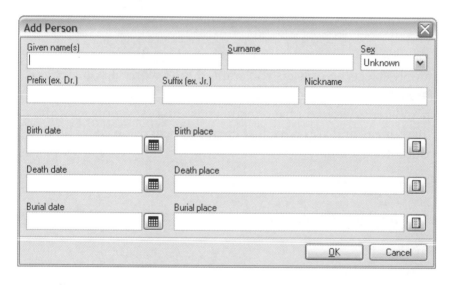

Let's start by adding your own information to the database that you just created. Select **"Add, Individual"** from the main menu, or click the "Add" button on the toolbar (it looks like the button to the left) and then select "Individual". This will bring up a screen where you can add your basic information.

Simply fill in the blanks, using the **Tab** or **Enter** key to move on to the next field. If you don't know some of the information, just leave the field empty. If you make a mistake, you can move back to the previous field by pressing **Shift+Tab** or by clicking the mouse on the field you want to move to.

Enter your given names (first, middle, etc) in the Given name(s) field. Separate each name with a space, like: **John Michael.**

The Surname field is where you will enter your last name. If you are female, you should enter your maiden (birth) name here.

Enter your sex in the Sex field by typing **M** or **F** as appropriate.
RootsMagic also supports Unknown as an option, but hopefully
you won't need to make that selection here.

You can also enter any prefix that should come before your name
(like "Dr."), any suffix that would come after your name (like
"Jr."), and any nickname you are known by (we won't even go
there).

You can also enter your birth date and birthplace. Enter the date
in just about any format you want, and RootsMagic will convert it
to the format you selected when you created the database. When
you enter the birthplace, enter it from specific to general with a
comma to separate each part of the place, like this:

Albuquerque, Bernalillo Co., New Mexico

Feel free to leave the death and burial fields blank here, since you
aren't dead (or buried). Click the **OK** button, and you should see
the data entry screen for yourself, with your name, sex and birth
information filled out.

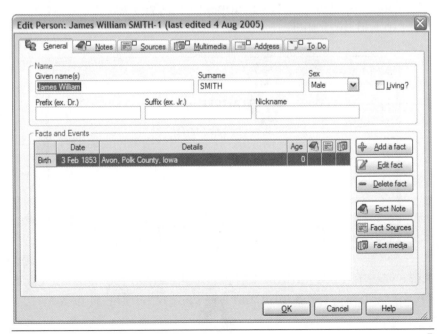

From this screen you can edit the information you just entered, or add other facts (like graduation, occupation, etc), notes, sources (documentation), to do items, multimedia items, and your current address. Add as much information as you want, and if you forget anything you can always come back later to add or change the information. For now, just click OK to finish adding yourself.

Adding Other People

One of the nice things about RootsMagic is that when you add a person to your database, it links the people together at the same time. Notice that when you press the arrow keys on the keyboard, or click on a person's name on the main pedigree view, the highlight bar moves to that person.

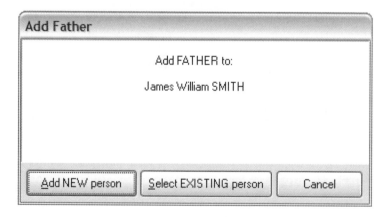 **To add your parents** to your database, make sure your name is highlighted on the main screen (by clicking your mouse on it), then select **"Add, Parents"** from the main menu, or click the "Add" button on the toolbar, then select "Parents".

The following dialog box will appear to let you select how you want to add the father.

Add Father

Add FATHER to:

James William SMITH

Add NEW person | Select EXISTING person | Cancel

Since your father's information is not already in the database click on the **"Add new person"** button and add your father the same way you added yourself. After you have added your father, you will go through the exact same steps to add your mother.

Once you have entered your parents, RootsMagic will ask if you want to add a marriage event for them. If your parents were married, select **"Yes"** (even if you don't know the date, place, or anything else about the marriage). RootsMagic will never assume a couple is married unless you add a marriage event. If you don't add the marriage event here, you can always add it later.

To add a spouse to your database, highlight the person you want to add the spouse to (by clicking your mouse on the person's name in the tree), then select **"Add, Spouse"** from the main menu, or click the "Add" button on the toolbar and select "Spouse".

Adding a spouse is exactly the same as adding your parents. You will get to choose between adding a new person or linking to an existing person. You will also be asked if you want to add a marriage event for this couple.

If you want to add additional spouses to a person, just repeat these steps for each spouse.

To enter an unmarried couple, you will still use the **"Add, Spouse"** command but just won't add a marriage event.

To add children to your database, highlight either the father or the mother, then select **"Add, Children"** from the main menu, or click the "Add" button on the toolbar and select "Children".

Once again, you will get the option to add a new person, or link to an existing person. This time the dialog will look a little bit different.

Since the person may have more than one spouse, the add child dialog will also ask which family to add the child to, and will also provide an option to add the child to the person and a new spouse. Highlight the family you want to add the child to then choose whether to add a new child or select an existing child.

When you finish adding a child, RootsMagic will display the family members and ask if you want to add another child to the same family. If you select **"Yes"**, you can simply repeat these steps to add more children.

When you have finished adding children, RootsMagic will bring up a list of the children in the family, and will ask you to arrange them in the proper birth order. Just use your mouse to drag and drop the children into the proper order, then click the **OK** button.

This child order is used when RootsMagic prints family group sheets, books, and other printouts where the children in a family are included.

That's all there is to it. Just highlight a person on the main screen and add a spouse, parents, or child to the person.

And now, on with the show…

The Main Screen

The views are wonderful from here.

One of the first things you may notice about RootsMagic is that
it offers three different navigation screens: the **Pedigree View**,
the **Family View**, and the **Descendants View**. To select one of
the views, simply click on the tabs at the top of the views, or
press the Tab key to switch between the views.

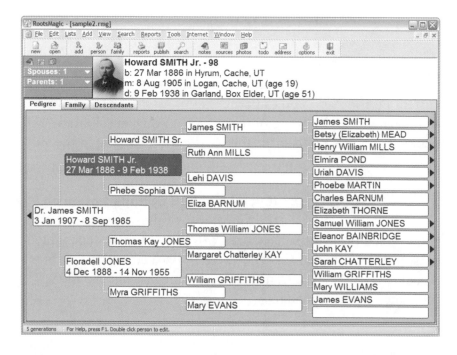

Above the tabs is an information area where RootsMagic
displays information about the currently highlighted person.
When you highlight a new person in any view, RootsMagic will
update this area with the person's picture, name, birth, marriage,
and death information.

A four line status area lies to the left of the information area.

 **The top row of the status area** will
display small icons if the highlighted

person has notes, sources, multimedia items, addresses, or to-do items. If you click on the camera, envelope or todo note, RootsMagic will allow you to edit that item for the person. If you click on the note or source icon, a list of all notes (or sources) for the person will appear and you can select one to edit.

Spouses: 2 ▼   **The second row of the status area** shows how many spouses the current person has. You can click on this area to bring up a list of the spouses and children with each spouse. You can select any person from this list to make them the current person in the view.

Parents: 1 ▼   **The third row of the status area** shows how many sets of parents the current person has. You can click on this area to bring up a list of the parents and siblings of the person. You can select any person from this list to make them the current person in the view.

LDS: BEPS   **If you have LDS options turned on**, the fourth row of the status area will show which ordinances have been completed for the highlighted person (B = baptized, E = endowed, P = sealed to parents, S = sealed to spouse). You can click on this area to edit the LDS ordinances for the person.

The Pedigree View

The "Pedigree View" displays a five generation ancestor tree of your family.

As you add individuals to your database, RootsMagic fills out the tree for you. You can move from person to person using the arrow keys on your keyboard, or by clicking on a person's name with the mouse.

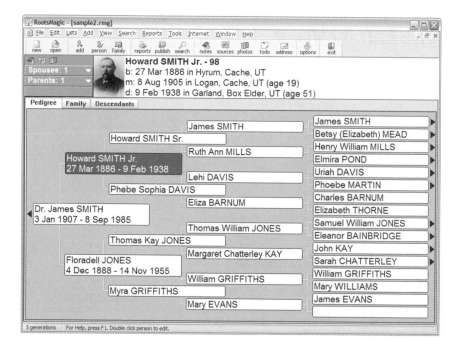

Once you have entered more generations than will fit on screen, RootsMagic will add small arrow buttons next to names to show that there are more individuals you can move to. Just click your mouse on one of these arrows and RootsMagic will scroll the next generation onto the screen. You can also just press an arrow key in the appropriate direction to scroll to another generation.

At the left side of the status bar (at the bottom of the screen) you will see "5 generations" displayed. You can click this area switch between displaying 5 and 6 generations on the screen at once.

You can edit any person in the Pedigree View by double clicking your mouse on the person's name, or you can simply highlight a person and press the Enter key.

The Family View

The "Family View" displays the father, mother, children and grandparents in a family. You can move from person to person using the arrow keys on your keyboard, or by clicking on a person's name with the mouse.

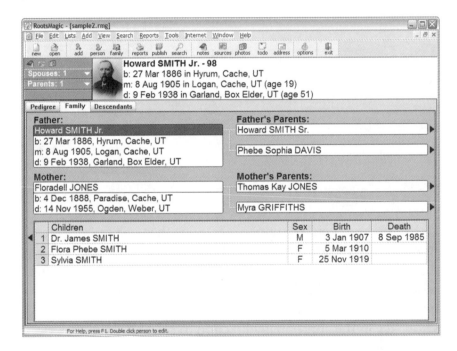

If grandparents are entered, a small arrow will appear to the right of the grandparent's name. Clicking your mouse on one of these arrows will move the grandparents into the parent position in the view.

RootsMagic will also add an arrow to the left of any child in the Family View who is married (or has a partner). Clicking your mouse on one of these arrows will change the view to the family where the child is an adult.

If the father or mother has additional spouses, a button labeled "other spouses" will appear above their name. You can click this button to display a list of the person's spouses, and you can change to a different spouse from the list.

Like in the Pedigree View, you can edit any person by double clicking your mouse on the person's name, or you can simply highlight a person and press the Enter key.

The Descendants View

The "Descendants View" displays a five generation indented descendancy of your family. The children of each person in the list are displayed under the parents, and are indented a small amount.

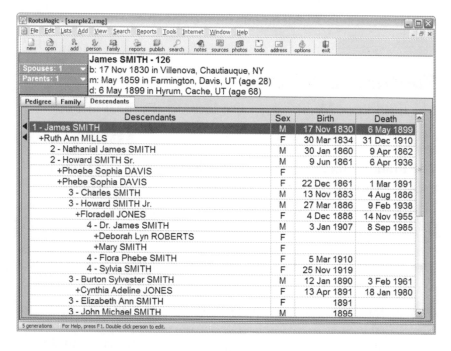

If the first person in the Descendants View has parents entered, an arrow will appear to the left of their name. You can click on this arrow (or press the left arrow key when the person is highlighted) to move one generation back in time.

In addition, RootsMagic will put an arrow to the left of any spouse who has parents entered as well, so that you can navigate to that part of the family. And before you ask why some people in the list **don't** have left arrows next to their names, it is because their parents are already displayed in the list (and pressing the left arrow key while they are highlighted will move to their parents).

If any person in the fifth generation has children, an arrow will be displayed to the right of their information. Clicking that arrow (or pressing the right arrow on the keyboard while they are highlighted) will scroll forward one generation in time to display that person's children.

At the left side of the status bar (at the bottom of the screen) you will see "5 generations". You can click this area and choose to display 2 through 7 generations on the screen at once.

Toolbars and Menus

The main RootsMagic screen also includes the main menu, a toolbar, and a status bar.

The main menu is where you will select most of the commands used by RootsMagic. The commands in the main menu are described in more detail in the chapter titled Quick Summary (page 265).

The toolbar is the row of buttons directly under the main menu.

These buttons are shortcuts for some of the commands in the main menu. If you move your mouse pointer over any of the buttons without clicking the mouse, a small yellow box (called a tool tip) will pop up and tell you what that button does.

You can customize the toolbar, by adding or deleting buttons, or rearranging the order of the buttons. Right click your mouse button on the toolbar, and then click on the "Customize" menu, and the following dialog will appear.

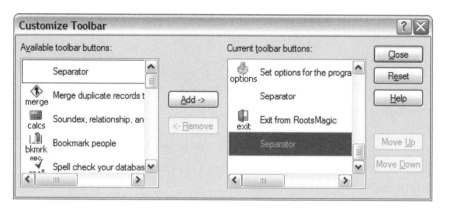

You can highlight a button in the "Available toolbar buttons" list and click the "Add ->" button to add the button to your toolbar. You can also highlight a button in the "Current toolbar buttons" list and click the "<- Remove" button to remove a button from your toolbar. You can even click and drag toolbar buttons between the lists, or click and drag buttons in the "Current" list to rearrange their order. And finally, if you totally mess things up, you can click the "Reset" button to restore the toolbar back to its default state.

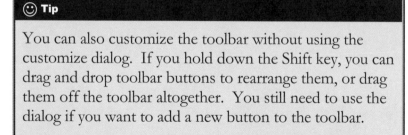

😊 Tip

You can also customize the toolbar without using the customize dialog. If you hold down the Shift key, you can drag and drop toolbar buttons to rearrange them, or drag them off the toolbar altogether. You still need to use the dialog if you want to add a new button to the toolbar.

You can also do "Tools, Options" from the menu, and then select the "Main screen" option. You will find a button to customize the toolbar, and another to choose from several different toolbar button styles.

The status bar is a bar across the bottom of the RootsMagic screen which displays various pieces of information.

In the Pedigree and Descendant views, the left side of the status bar will display how many generations are currently displayed on screen. You can click this area to change the number of generations displayed.

The status bar can also display the relationship of the highlighted person to any selected person in your database. This feature is described on page 225.

And finally, when you move your mouse pointer over a toolbar button, a longer description of that command will appear in the status bar.

Using Databases

It is a capital mistake to theorize before one has data.
- Sir Arthur Conan Doyle

The heart of any genealogy software is the database engine, and RootsMagic is no exception. A RootsMagic database can hold up to 2 billion individuals, so a single database can easily hold all the family members you can enter.

If you *do* want to separate your information into different databases, RootsMagic will allow you to have as many databases as will fit on your hard disk.

> ☺ **Tip**
>
> It is usually best to enter your entire family in a single database so that charts, relationship calculator, searches, etc are able to operate on the entire family structure.

Creating a New Database

Before you can do anything in RootsMagic, you must tell it to create a new database to store your information in.

To create a new database select **"File, New"** from the main menu or click the "New" button on the toolbar. RootsMagic will ask you to enter the name of the new database using the standard Windows file dialog. Simply enter the filename (and select which folder you want the database in) and click the **OK** button and the following dialog box will appear.

Date format determines how RootsMagic will display dates you enter. You can actually enter dates in just about any format and RootsMagic will automatically convert them to the format you select here.

Number to display after name on main screen lets you choose whether RootsMagic displays the program assigned record number after a person's name, or a user entered reference number, or no number at all.

Display surnames uppercase lets you tell RootsMagic whether you want it to display and print surnames (last names) in all uppercase.

LDS support enables or disables the printing of LDS (Mormon) information on printouts and certain other LDS features.

Simply select the options you want. Don't worry if you aren't sure which settings you want to use. You can always change them later. After you have made your choices, click the OK button, and you have just created a new database to hold your information.

Opening an Existing Database

 If you have created more than one database, you will need to be able to access the different databases. Clicking the "Open" button on the toolbar, or selecting **"File, Open"** from the main menu will let you select which database you want to use.

RootsMagic will keep track of the most recently used databases, so that you can select one without searching for it. Just select "File" from the main menu, and select one of the files listed near the bottom of the menu.

If you can't find one of your databases, select "File, Search" from the main menu. The following dialog will appear.

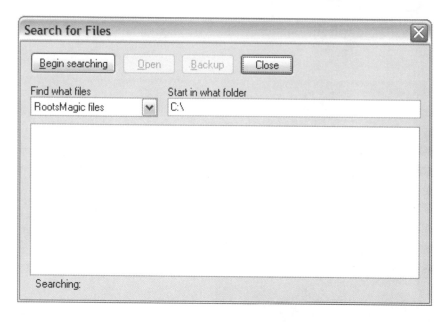

Just tell RootsMagic what type of file to search for (RootsMagic, Family Origins, PAF or GEDCOM files), and which folder to start in, and then click the "Begin searching" button. RootsMagic will search your hard drive and will list all the RootsMagic files it finds. You can then highlight any of the files in the list and click the "Open" button to open that file. You can also click the "Backup" button to create a backup of the highlighted file.

If you want to close a database, just select "File, Close" from the main menu. If you have more than one database open (we'll talk about that in the next section), make sure you have selected the database you want to close so RootsMagic knows which one you want closed. The selected database is simply the last one you clicked on or were moving around in.

Using Multiple Databases

RootsMagic allows you to have more than one database open on screen at the same time. These can be totally different databases, or multiple copies of the same database. Just open (or create) the additional databases exactly the same way you did the first, and RootsMagic will automatically place the two databases side by side on the screen.

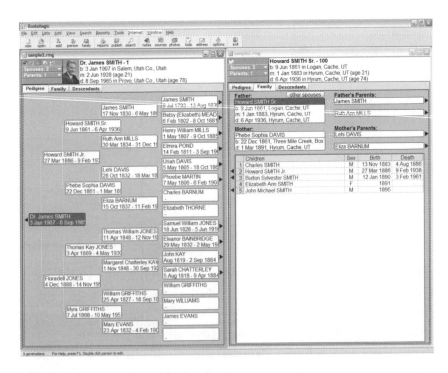

You may have up to 9 databases open at once (although the screen gets really crowded if you do). Each database window acts independently from the others, so you can even view different parts of the same database using two different views at the same time.

Dragging and Dropping People

If you have two different databases open at the same time, RootsMagic will let you drag and drop people from one database to the other. Dragging and dropping a person copies them to the new database, and does not remove them from the original database.

Simply click your mouse on a person in one database (in any of the main views), and while holding the mouse button down, drag the person to the other database. RootsMagic will bring up the following screen in case you want to copy more than just that one person.

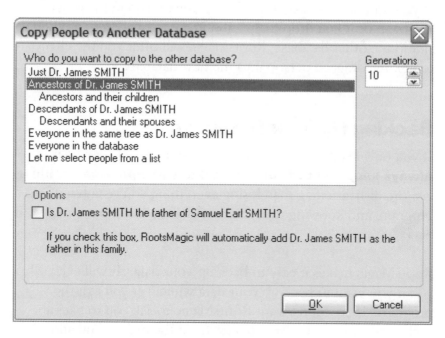

You can select which people you want to drag from one database to the other. Your options are:

➢ **Just the person** you dragged.
➢ **Ancestors of the person** copies the direct ancestors (parents, grandparents, etc) of the person you dragged. You can enter the number of generations to copy. You can also select to have the children of the ancestors copied as well.
➢ **Descendants of the person** copies the direct descendants (children, grandchildren, etc) of the person you dragged. You can enter the number of generations to copy. You can also select to have the spouses of descendants copied as well.
➢ **Everyone in the same tree as the person** copies everyone related to the person you dragged.
➢ **Everyone in the database** copies the entire database.
➢ **Let me select people from a list** brings up the selection screen (page 181) where you can select any group of people to copy.

If you drop a person on top of the same person in the other database, or if you drop the person in an empty parent or child slot in the other database, RootsMagic will offer you the chance to link the dragged person into the new database.

Backing Up Your Database

If you only learn one thing from this book, this should be it. **Always keep a set of current backups of your data.** Nothing is more disheartening than losing everything you've entered into a program, and knowing that you don't have a backup copy of your data.

RootsMagic makes it easy to back up your data. It will even ask you if you want to back up your data whenever you exit the program. If you don't want RootsMagic to ask you to backup each time you exit, do "Tools, Options" from the main menu and uncheck that option. To back up your data at any other time, do

"File, Backup" from the main menu. RootsMagic will back up the currently selected database.

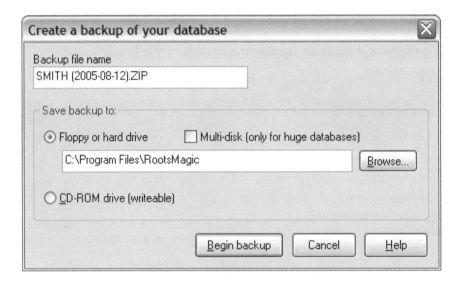

RootsMagic will display a default backup file name which includes the current day's date so you can easily keep multiple backups.

A working RootsMagic database is made up of 30+ files. When you back up your database RootsMagic zips those files up into a single backup file with a .zip extension.

You can save your backup to a floppy or hard drive, or to a CD-ROM drive (if it is a writeable drive). If you back up to a floppy or the hard drive, you can enter the drive letter and full path name where you want the backup to be written. If you save the backup to your CD-ROM burner, RootsMagic will replace anything already on the CD with your backup.

A special option is available when writing to a floppy drive. Sometimes your backup is too large to fit on a single floppy. When that happens you can mark the checkbox called "Multi-disk" and RootsMagic will write the backup across multiple floppies. If you need to use this option, make sure you label each of your backup disks like DISK1, DISK2, etc so that you know the order RootsMagic will want them if you ever need to restore the backup. This option does not work when backing up to a fixed drive (like your hard disk).

To restore a backed up database, select "File, Restore" from the main menu.

Enter the name of the backup to restore (it will have a .zip extension), or click the "Browse" button to select from the file dialog. Then enter the folder you want RootsMagic to restore the backup into. The restored database will have the same name as it had originally. If there is already a database with that name in the directory you choose, RootsMagic will ask if you want to overwrite the existing database. After RootsMagic restores the backup files, it will open the newly restored database.

> **Note**
>
> While RootsMagic's backup feature will back up links to multimedia items, it does not back up any of the multimedia items themselves (photos, sound or video clips). Those items are often in other directories, or even scattered around in multiple directories. You will want to back those multimedia items up separately.

While a single backup copy of each database is better than no backup, some backup techniques can provide even more protection.

When creating a backup, try not to always overwrite your previous backup. It is sometimes possible to have corruption in your database without knowing it and your backup could contain a corrupted database. By having multiple backups you can go back to earlier backups that may have been created before the corruption occurred.

Renaming Your Database

If you ever need to rename your database make sure you use the **"File, Rename"** command. It will simply ask you for the new database name. **Never** try to rename the database from Windows or a DOS prompt. It may result in you not being able to access your database anymore.

Deleting Your Database

Here is a command you should never use on your database, unless you are absolutely sure you don't need it anymore. The **"File, Delete"** command will completely remove the current database from your hard disk. RootsMagic will ask you to verify that you really want to do this.

Copying Your Database

The **"File, Copy"** command lets you create an exact copy of your database. You can choose what folder and filename you want for the copy. This command can be useful if you want to make a copy of your database that you can make temporary changes to without affecting your main database.

If you want to back up your database, you should use the "File, Backup" command from the menu instead since it compresses your database into a single file which can be transported more easily.

Rebuilding Your Indexes

Your database contains files called "indexes" which help tell RootsMagic how data is linked together. For example, which people are linked to which families, which events are linked to which people, etc.

If your indexes ever become corrupted for some reason, RootsMagic can rebuild those indexes for you. If you ever notice people becoming linked to events or other people that you didn't link them too, it may be time to rebuild your indexes.

To rebuild your indexes select "File, Rebuild indexes" from the main menu. The following dialog will appear, offering some additional options.

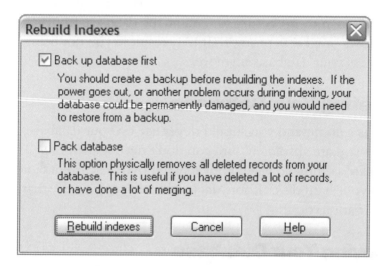

➢ **Back up database first** – If your computer hangs or the power goes out while you are reindexing or packing, your data will probably be trashed. It is always wise to make sure you have a backup before performing this function.

➢ **Pack database** - Any time you delete a record (whether it is a person, note, source, etc), or do a merge (which deletes one of the records after merging), RootsMagic will mark the record as deleted, but does not shrink the file to reuse the deleted space. Checking this option will regenerate your database files, removing all deleted records and compressing the database to reclaim the space.

Getting Database Information

The "File, Properties" command displays information about the current database, including the full path name, and the number of records (people, families, sources, places, etc) in the database.

Building the Family Tree

Every time I find an ancestor, I need to find two more.

Adding People to Your Database

As with most database programs, RootsMagic allows you to enter new information from the keyboard or by importing data from existing files.

> **Note**
>
> If you are lucky enough to already have data in a GEDCOM, PAF, or Family Origins file, then you will want to read the chapter titled "Sharing Data with Others" (page 190).

To add individuals to your RootsMagic database, use one of the four **"Add"** commands from the main menu, or click the "Add" toolbar button.

The **"Add, Individual" command** simply lets you add an unlinked person to your database. The first person you add to a database must be added this way, since there is nobody to add parents, spouses, or children to yet.

The **"Add, Parents" command** adds parents to the person who is highlighted on the main screen. You can add more than one set of parents to each person.

The **"Add, Spouse" command** adds a spouse (or unmarried partner) to the person who is highlighted on the main screen. You can multiple spouses to each person.

The **"Add, Child" command** adds a child to the person who is highlighted on the main screen. When adding children to a family, you may want to switch to the Family View to get a clearer picture of the family unit.

As you add a person to your database, RootsMagic will automatically link the person and add their name to the main views.

> **✎ Note**
>
> The RootsMagic "Add" commands are consistent in that they **always** add to the highlighted person. For example, if you highlight a child in the Family View and do **"Add, Child"**, the child will be added to the highlighted person, and **not** as a child in the displayed family.

Adding an Unlinked Individual

To add an unlinked individual, click the **"Add"** button on the toolbar (it looks like the button to the left) and then select "Individual"", or do **"Add, Individual"** from the main menu. You can also just press the letter "I" on the keyboard as a shortcut. This will bring up a screen where you can add the basic information for the person.

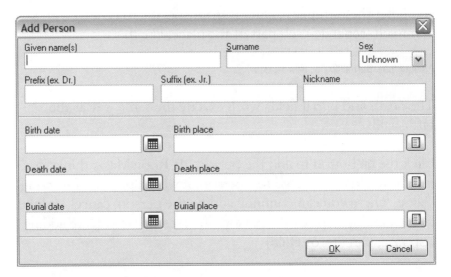

Simply fill in the blanks, using the **Tab** or **Enter** key to move on to the next field. If you don't know some of the information, just leave the field empty. If you make a mistake, you can move back to the previous field by pressing Shift+Tab or by clicking the mouse on the field you want to move to.

Enter your given names (first, middle, etc) in the Given name(s) field. Separate each name with a space, like: John Michael.

The Surname field is where you will enter your last name. If you are female, you should enter your maiden (birth) name here.

Enter your sex in the Sex field by typing M or F as appropriate. RootsMagic also supports Unknown as an option, but hopefully you won't need to make that selection here.

You can also enter any prefix that should come before your name (like "Dr."), any suffix that would come after your name (like "Jr."), and any nickname you are known by (we won't even go there).

You can also enter your birth date and birthplace. Enter the date in just about any format you want, and RootsMagic will convert it to the format you selected when you created the database. When you enter the birthplace, enter it from specific to general with a comma to separate each part of the place, like this:

Albuquerque, Bernalillo Co., New Mexico

The death and burial fields work exactly the same way as the birth fields.

Click the OK button to add the person. If RootsMagic thinks you may have already entered this person, it will display the following dialog, where you can continue adding the person, cancel, or link to the existing copy of the person (in cases where you are adding a spouse, parents, or child).

RootsMagic will then bring up the data entry screen for the new person, with the name, sex and birth, death and burial information filled out.

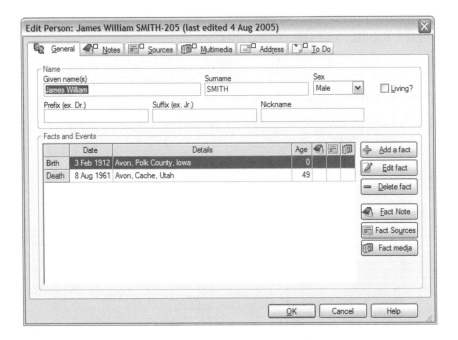

From this screen you can edit existing information, add other facts (like graduation, occupation, etc), notes, sources (documentation), to do items, scrapbook items, and your current address. Add as many items as you want, and if you forget anything, you can always come back later to add or change the information. This edit screen is described in more detail in the next chapter titled "Editing People" (page 38).

When you are satisfied with your entries, click OK to finish adding the unlinked individual.

Adding Parents, Spouses, and Children

One of the nice things about RootsMagic is that when you add a person to your database, it links the people together at the same time. Notice that when you press the arrow keys on the keyboard, or click on a person's name on the main pedigree chart, the highlight bar moves to that person.

To add parents to someone in your database, highlight the name of the person on the main screen (by clicking your mouse on it), then press "P" on the keyboard, or click the **"Add"** button on the toolbar and select "Parents".

The following dialog box will appear to let you select how you want to add the father.

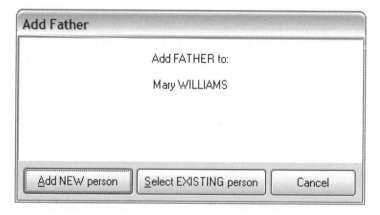

> **Add new person** allows you to add the father's record to the database from scratch. If you click this button, you will add the father exactly the same way you add an unlinked individual.

➢ **Select existing person** is available in case the father's information is already in the database. If you click this button, a list of everybody in the database will appear, and you can select the father from the list.

➢ **Cancel** lets you cancel adding the father. This is useful if you don't want to add parents after all, or if you don't know the father but still want to add a mother.

After you have added the father, you will go through the exact same steps to add the mother.

Once you have entered the parents, RootsMagic will ask if you want to add a marriage event for them. If the parents were married, select **"Yes"** (even if you don't know the date, place, or anything else about the marriage). RootsMagic will never assume a couple is married unless you add a marriage event. If you don't add the marriage event here, you can always add it later.

You can add additional sets of parents to a person by repeating these steps. This allows you to track natural, adopted, foster, or any other types of relationships.

To add a spouse (or unmarried partner) to someone in your database, highlight the person you want to add the spouse to (by clicking your mouse on the person's name in the tree), then press "S" on the keyboard, or click the **"Add"** button on the toolbar and select Spouse.

Adding a spouse is exactly the same as adding parents. You will get to choose between adding a new person or selecting an existing person. You will also be asked if you want to add a marriage event for this couple.

If you want to add multiple spouses to a person, just repeat these steps for each spouse.

When you encounter a situation where a couple has children but are not married, you will still use the **"Add, Spouse"** command but just won't add a marriage event.

To add a child to someone in your database, highlight either the father or the mother, then press "C" on the keyboard, or click the **"Add"** button on the toolbar and select "Child".

Once again, you will get the option to add a new person, or select an existing person. This time the dialog will look a little bit different.

Since the person may have more than one spouse, the add child dialog will also ask which family to add the child to, and will also provide an option to add the child to the person and a new spouse. Choose which family to add the child to and then add the new child or select an existing child.

When you finish adding a child, RootsMagic will display the family and ask if you want to add another child to the family. If you select **"Yes"**, you can simply repeat these steps to add more children.

Once you have finished adding children to the family, RootsMagic will bring up a list of the children in the family, and will ask you to arrange them in the proper birth order. Just use your mouse to drag and drop the children into the proper order, then click the **OK** button.

This child order is used when RootsMagic prints family group sheets, books, and other printouts where the children in a family are included.

Deleting People and Families

If you ever add someone to your database that you really didn't mean to, RootsMagic provides two commands to help you remove them.

To delete a person, highlight the person's name on the main screen, then do **"Edit, Delete, Person"** from the main menu. RootsMagic will ask if you want to delete the person.

When you delete a person, RootsMagic will unlink the person from all families and will remove the person's record, including facts, notes, source citations, multimedia links, and to do items.

> ☺ **Tip**
>
> Use the "File, Rebuild indexes" command with the "Pack database" option occasionally if you delete a lot of individuals. When you delete a person or family, RootsMagic doesn't automatically reuse the space in the database where the deleted record was. Packing your database will do this for you.

To delete a family, highlight either the father or the mother on the main screen, then do **"Edit, Delete, Family"** from the main menu. RootsMagic will display the family in the following dialog. RootsMagic offers two methods of deleting a family.

> **Unlink the family members from each other.** No other links will be broken, and the people will not be removed from the database. For example, the parents will still be linked to their parents and other spouses, and children will still be linked to their spouses and children. RootsMagic will also delete any marriage facts or notes associated with the family.

> **Delete all of the family members from the database.** RootsMagic will delete both parents and each child from the database.

☺ Tip

If you ever encounter a situation in your database where a person has an "Unknown" spouse that you can't seem to get rid of, bring up the family with the unknown spouse in the Family View on the main screen, highlight the parent that isn't "Unknown" and do the **"Edit, Delete, Family"** command. Select the option to "Unlink the people as a family" and RootsMagic will remove the "Unknown" spouse.

Unlinking People from Each Other

There will come a time when you will link a person into your family the wrong way. It is not uncommon to accidentally link a person as his own grandfather.

Unlinking a person from their spouse unlinks them as a parent in the currently displayed family. Highlight the person you want to unlink, making sure that the spouse you want to unlink from is also displayed on the screen. Then select **"Edit, Unlink, from Spouse"** from the main menu. Only the link to the currently displayed spouse and children will be broken. All other links will remain intact, including links to parents and other spouses.

Unlinking a person from their parents unlinks them as a child in the currently displayed family. Highlight the person you want to unlink, making sure that the parents you want to unlink from are also displayed on the screen. Then select **"Edit, Unlink, from Parents"** from the main menu. Only the link to the currently displayed parents will be broken. All other links will remain intact, including links to spouses and other sets of parents (if any).

> ☺ **Tip**
>
> If you need to change the sex field for a person, you will need to unlink them from any spouses before you can change the sex.

Swapping Husbands and Wives

This isn't what it sounds like. There are times when you may enter a husband and wife backwards. This may be a situation where you couldn't tell the sex based on the name (Kim and Francis Smith), or it may just be accidental. RootsMagic has a command which will let you switch the husband and the wife in a family without having to unlink them first. Just highlight either the husband or wife, and select **"Edit, Swap husband and wife"** from the main menu.

Editing People

History is only a confused heap of facts. - Lord Chesterfield

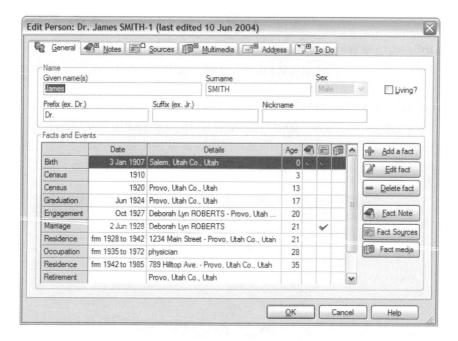

The RootsMagic edit screen is the place where you will enter everything you know about a person. To edit a person, simply double click on the person's name on the main screen. You can also highlight the person on the main screen and press the **Enter** key to bring up the edit screen.

If you want the edit screen to be a little larger, you can resize it by clicking the edge of the edit screen and dragging it.

Names, Titles and Sex

The top section of the edit screen contains fields where you can just type in the person's name, titles and sex. When you finish filling in one field, you can move to the next field by pressing the **Enter** or **Tab** key. If you make a mistake, you can press **Shift+Tab** to move back to the previous field. You can also click your mouse on any field to move the cursor there for editing.

The Given names field is where you enter the person's given names (first, middle, etc). You should separate each given name with a space, like this: John Michael.

The Surname field is where you enter the person's last name. If the person is female, you should enter their maiden (unmarried) name here.

The Sex field is a list that you can select "Male", "Female" or "Unknown" from. You can click your mouse on the list and select the sex, or press the first letter of the sex ("M", "F", or "U"). If the person has a spouse entered, then the sex field will be disabled so you can't change it. If you need to change the sex field, you need to unlink the person from any spouse(s) before trying to change the sex.

The Prefix field provides a place to enter titles that come *before* the person's name, such as *Dr.* John Smith.

The Suffix field provides a place to enter titles that come *after* the person's name, such as John Smith *Jr.*

The Nickname field provides a place to enter a nickname that the person was (or is) known by.

The Living checkbox lets you mark whether the person is still living. This is used if you choose to "privatize" data for living people when creating GEDCOM files or websites.

Facts and Events

RootsMagic allows you to enter unlimited facts to each person. A fact can be **an event** like a birth or death, **a phase in the person's life** like an occupation or military service, or **a descriptive item** like an ID number or physical description.

A fact can contain a date (or date period), a place, a description if necessary, a note, pictures and unlimited source citations.

You can enter multiple copies of each fact type, so you can, for example, enter all 10 occupations in Uncle Joe's life. By adding all these facts (along with fact notes and fact sources) you are building a complete personal history for each person in your database.

Adding a Fact to a Person

To add a fact to an individual, click the **"Add Fact"** button on the person's edit screen, or press **Alt+A** as a shortcut key. RootsMagic will display a list of fact types that you can choose from.

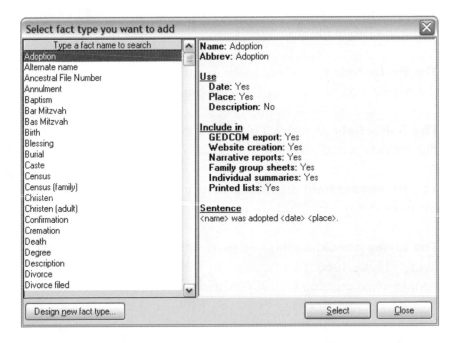

Simply highlight the type of fact you want to add. As with any list in RootsMagic, you can use the arrow keys to highlight the item, or can just begin typing the fact name and RootsMagic will move to the matching fact type for you.

If you want to add a fact that isn't in the list, you can
create your own fact types. This is discussed in the next
chapter titled "Facts and Events" (page 48).

Once you have highlighted the type of fact you want to add to
the person, just click the **Select** button and RootsMagic will bring
up a dialog where you can enter the details for the new fact. You
can enter the date and place for the fact, as well as a note,
sources, or multimedia objects.

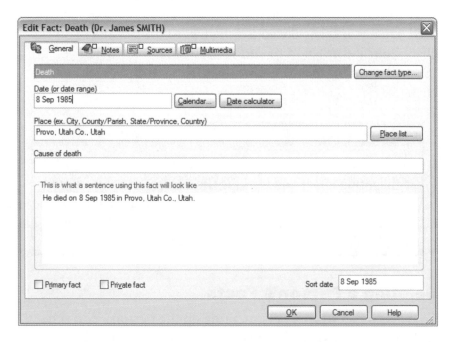

Simply fill in the information you know then click the OK button
to save the new fact. Don't worry if you don't know some of the
information. Just enter as much as you can. You can always
come back to make changes or add more information. The "Edit
Fact" dialog is described in more detail in the chapter titled
"Facts and Events" (page 48).

If you have "conflicting" information about a fact (for example, two different birth dates), you can enter two different birth facts to the person, and use the "Primary fact" checkbox to tell RootsMagic which fact is the main one to use.

For more information on facts and how they work, see the next chapter titled "Facts and Events" (page 48).

Editing a Person's Facts

To edit a fact for a person, bring up the person's edit screen, click your mouse on the fact you want to edit, then click the **"Edit Fact"** button (or simply click your mouse on the name of the fact you want to edit). RootsMagic will display the same dialog that you used when you originally added the fact to the person. You can change any information or add new information. When you are satisfied with the changes, click the OK button to save the changes.

☺ **Tip**

Here's a shortcut for editing a fact note. Instead of highlighting a fact and clicking the **"Fact Note"** button, simply click on the little box next to the fact in the note column. This also works for editing fact sources and multimedia scrapbooks.

Deleting a Person's Facts

To delete a fact from a person, bring up the person's edit screen, click your mouse on the fact you want to delete, then click the **"Delete Fact"** button. RootsMagic will ask you to confirm that you really want to delete the fact. Click **"Yes"** to remove the fact from the person's list.

Other Pages – Notes, Sources, and More

At the top of each person's edit screen are tabs which let you add or edit other information for the person; a general note, general source citations, a multimedia scrapbook, the person's current address, and their to do list. Simply click any of the tabs to add or edit any of this information. If information is already entered in any of these areas, the little box on the tab will be filled red.

General Notes

The "Notes" tab lets you enter and edit the "general" note for the person. This is a note that is associated with the person, but not specific to any particular fact you have entered for them (you would use the fact notes for that purpose). For details on notes, see the chapter titled "Notes – Telling Your Story" (page 71).

General Sources

The "Sources" tab lets you enter and edit the "general" sources for the person. These are sources that are associated with the person, but not specific to any particular fact you have entered for them (you would use the fact sources for that purpose). For details on sources, see the chapter titled "Sources – Proving It" (page 75).

Multimedia Scrapbook

The "Multimedia" tab shows the multimedia scrapbook for the person. The multimedia scrapbook allows you to enter and scan photos for a person, and attach documents, sound and video clips to a person. Photos attached to a person can be printed in many of RootsMagic's reports and charts. For more information on the multimedia scrapbook, see the chapter titled "Pictures, Sound, and Video" (page 89).

Address

The "Address" tab lets you enter and edit the current addresses for the person. You only need to enter an address for the head of a household, not for each person in the household. This address is intended only for the "current" address. You can add "Resided" facts to the person if you want to track all the places the person ever lived. These addresses can be printed in the form of an address list or address labels, or can be exported to a mail-merge file that you can import into your word processor. The address page works exactly the same as the "Repository" page described on page 86.

To Do List

The "To Do" tab shows the to do list for the person. The to-do list provides a place to save all those tasks you need to accomplish for the person. For details on the to do list, see the chapter titled "Research Aids" (page 211).

Editing a Family

If you cannot get rid of the family skeleton, you may as well make it dance. —George Bernard Shaw

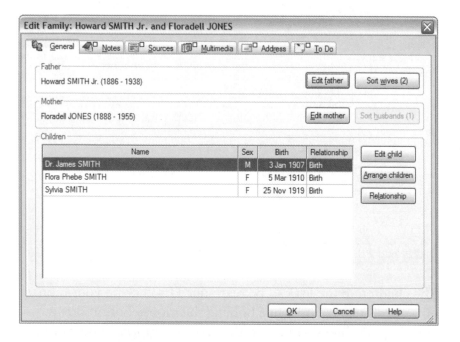

The Edit Family screen provides a single location where you can edit information about a single family (dad, mom, and the kids).

To edit family information, highlight the father or mother on the main screen and press **Ctrl+Enter** key, or select **"Edit, family"** from the main menu.

Editing Family Members

You can edit any family member using the "Edit father", "Edit mother", or "Edit Child" buttons. RootsMagic will open the edit screen for the person (described in the previous chapter). The "Edit Child" button lets you edit whichever child is highlighted in the list of children.

Child Relationships

There are a number of different relationships a child can have in a family, and RootsMagic allows you to set that relationship for each child in the family. Highlight any child in the list and click the Relationship button. You can choose from birth, adopted, foster, sealing, step, challenged, or disproved.

Rearranging Children

To rearrange the children in the family by birth date, click the "Arrange children" button, and the following dialog will appear.

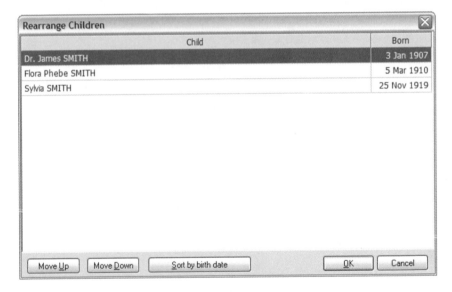

The children in the list can be rearranged by clicking your mouse on a child's name, and while holding the mouse button down, dragging the child's name into the proper position. You can also rearrange a person by using the highlighting the person, then clicking the "Move up" or "Move down" buttons. Repeat this for each child that needs to be rearranged, and then click the OK button to close the child list.

You can also click the "Sort by birth date" button to have RootsMagic automatically rearrange the children by their birth date.

Rearranging Spouses

To rearrange a person's spouses by marriage date, click either the "Sort wives" or "Sort husbands" button. The buttons will show how many spouses the person has. If the person does not have multiple spouses, the button will be grayed out. A list of spouses similar to the list of children in the previous section will appear.

The spouses in the list can be rearranged by clicking your mouse on a spouse's name, and while holding the mouse button down, dragging the spouse's name into the proper position. Repeat this for each spouse that needs to be rearranged, then click the OK button to close the spouse list.

Family Notes, Photos, and Other Stuff

At the top of each family's edit screen are tabs which let you add or edit other information for the family; a family note, family source citations, a multimedia scrapbook, the family's current address, and their to do list. Simply click any of the tabs to add or edit any of this information. If information is already entered in any of these areas, the little box on the tab will be filled red. These pages are exactly the same as those described in "Editing People" on page 43.

Facts and Events

History is only a confused heap of facts. - Lord Chesterfield

What Is a Fact?

RootsMagic allows you to track every detail in a person's life in the form of "facts". A fact can be **an event** like a birth or death, **a phase in the person's life** like an occupation or military service, or **a descriptive item** like an ID number or physical description.

When you add or edit a fact RootsMagic will display the "Edit Fact" dialog where you can enter the information for the fact. A fact can contain of any or all of the following parts: a date (or date period), a place, a description, a note, unlimited source citations, and multimedia items (like pictures).

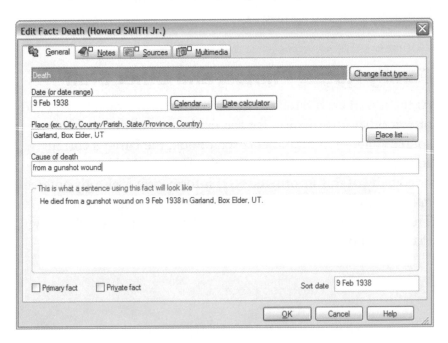

You can also choose whether a fact is a primary or private fact. **A primary fact** is useful when you have multiple facts of the same type (like more than one birth fact when you have

conflicting information). **A private fact** is one you may not
want included in reports or other uses. Most reports offer the
option to print or ignore private facts.

Dates

RootsMagic will accept just about any date you type, and will
convert it into a standard format for displaying and printing.
While you should enter the full date (day, month and year) if you
know it, RootsMagic will also accept partial dates, like **"Feb 1780"**, **"13
Feb"**, **"Feb"**, or **"1780"**. You can even use BC if you are lucky enough
to have information back that far.

RootsMagic also supports double dates, which was used in
England prior to the adoption of the Gregorian calendar. You
would enter these double dates with a slash separating the 2
years, like **"13 Feb 1729/30"**.

RootsMagic provides several **date modifiers**, which you can add
to your dates to alter their meaning. You can use them with full
dates, partial dates, or a combination of the two.

"Before" means that the fact happened before this date. You
can enter the date in any of these formats: **"before 10 May 1959"**, **"bef 10
May 1959"** or **"b 10 May 1959"**.

"About" means that the fact happened around this date. You can
enter the date in any of these formats: **"about 10 May 1959"**, **"abt 10 May
1959"**, **"circa 10 May 1959"**, **"cir 10 May 1959"**, **"c 10 May 1959"**, or **"ca 10 May 1959"**.

"Estimated" means that you either guessed at the date, or
calculated the date based on other information. You can enter it
like **"estimated 10 May 1959"** or **"est 10 May 1959"**.

"Between/And" means that the fact happened somewhere
between these two dates. You can enter the dates in any of these

formats: **"between 10 May 1959 and 12 June 1959"** or **"bet 10 May 1959 and 12 June 1959"**.

"Or" means that the fact happened on one of these two dates. These dates would be entered like: **"10 May 1959 or 12 June 1959"**.

"From/To" means that the fact happened during the entire period between the two dates. This is useful for facts like Occupation and Military Service where the fact occurred during the entire period. You can enter the dates in any of these formats: **"from 10 May 1959 to 12 June 1959"**, **"frm 10 May 1959 to 12 June 1959"**, or **"fr 10 May 1959 to 12 June 1959"**.

"After" means that the fact happened after this date. You can enter this date in any of these formats: **"after 10 May 1959"**, **"aft 10 May 1959"**, or **"a 10 May 1959"**.

If you enter...	RootsMagic will display...
2/13/1780	13 Feb 1780
February 13	13 Feb
2/13/1779/80	13 Feb 1779/80
b 2/13/1780	before 13 Feb 1780
a 13-2-1780	after 13 Feb 1780
abt 1780	about 1780
2/1780 or 3/1780	Feb 1780 or Mar 1780
bet 2/1780 and 3/10/1780	between Feb 1780 and 10 Mar 1780
from 1/1/1780 to February 2, 1780	from 1 Jan 1780 to 2 Feb 1780
abt 100 bc	about 100 BC
August	Aug

And finally, even if you enter a date that RootsMagic doesn't understand (for example **"the second Tuesday after Easter"**), it will still accept the date.

The "Edit Fact" dialog also has two buttons available when working with dates. The "Calendar" button will pop up a calendar that you can select a date from, while the "Date calculator" button will bring up a calculator (page 227) which will let you perform date calculations.

Sort Dates

The sort date is a "non printing" date which you can enter to force RootsMagic to sort the facts in the order you want.

When you enter the normal date for the fact, RootsMagic will automatically fill the sort date, but you can change it if you want. This is useful in situations like when you have a death fact with a place but don't know the date. Instead of putting in a fake date like "after 1 Jan 1900" in the date field, you can go ahead and leave the date field blank but put in a sort date to force the fact into the position you desire. It must contain a day, month, and year part (all three).

Places

RootsMagic facts allow you to enter the place where the fact or event occurred. When you enter a place, separate each part with a comma, and enter it from specific to general like this:

Albuquerque, Bernalillo County, New Mexico

By separating each part of the place with a comma, RootsMagic can abbreviate the place when it needs to fit the place name in a tight area of a report.

> ☺ **Tip**
>
> When entering place names, it is best to spell out the different parts if there is enough room. While abbreviations like the post office abbreviations for states are standard in their country of origin, they are not standard throughout the rest of the world.

Every time you enter a new place, RootsMagic adds the place you enter to the **"Place List"**. Whenever you need to enter a place, RootsMagic will autofill the place as you type. As you type each letter of the place name, RootsMagic tries to match the letters you've typed with existing names in the Place List. Just continue typing characters until the correct place appears. You can also click the "Place list" button on the "Edit Fact" dialog to bring up a list of previously entered places to choose from.

RootsMagic allows you to make changes to the Place List by selecting **"Lists, Place list"** from the main menu. The following list will appear.

To edit a place in your place list, highlight the name of the place by clicking on it with your mouse, then click the **"Edit"** button. A dialog will appear where you can edit the place name, the latitude and longitude for the place (optional), and a note or place history for the place (also optional).

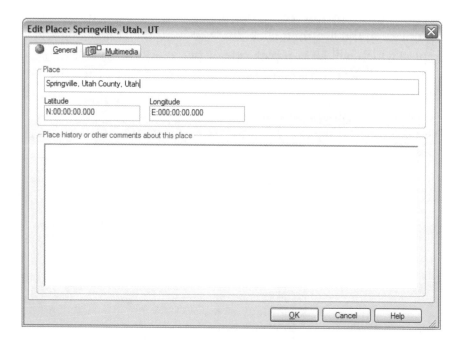

Just change the place name the way you want, then click the OK button to save the modified place name. Every fact that uses that place name will be adjusted to use the modified place name.

At some point you may find your place list cluttered with multiple copies of the same place, each spelled just a little differently. This is especially common after importing information from a GEDCOM file. If you edit a place name to look like another place in the list, RootsMagic will automatically merge the two place names together for you.

You can also click the "Multimedia" tab to open the scrapbook (described on page 89) for the highlighted place. This is useful for adding a picture of a home, cemetery plot, or other landmark to a place.

To delete a place in your place list, highlight the name of the place in the list, then click the **"Delete"** button. RootsMagic will ask if you really want to delete the place name. If you do delete the place name, any facts that happened in that place will have their place field erased.

To print information from your place list, highlight the name of a place in the list, then click the **"Print"** button. This dialog will appear which will let you pick one of two types of place list printouts. Select the type of printout you want, then click the OK button.

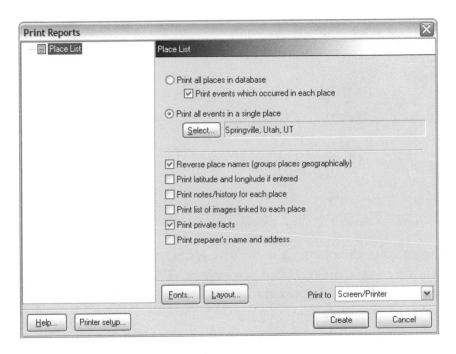

Print all places in database will print a list of every place in your database. You can also choose to have RootsMagic print all the events which occurred in each of those places.

Print all events in a single place will print a list of every fact in your database that occurred in the highlighted place. It will list the person's name, fact type, and date for each fact.

RootsMagic can also print the latitude and longitude (if entered), place notes or a list of images linked to each place. You can also use the "Print private facts" checkbox to tell RootsMagic whether to print facts that you have marked as private.

Descriptions

Some facts have what is called a "description". This is where you enter a specific detail about a fact. For example, in the Occupation fact, you would enter the actual occupation (for example **"teacher"**).

The Fact List

RootsMagic has a "fact list" with a number of built-in fact types that are already defined and include the appropriate fields. You can also create your own fact types that RootsMagic will add to the fact list. A description of each of these facts can be found in the Quick Summary at the end of this book.

You can get to the fact list in two different ways: 1) by clicking the **"Add Fact"** button on a person's edit screen, and 2) by selecting **"Lists, Fact type list"** from the main menu. You can scroll through the list of fact types and see details about the highlighted fact type on the right side of the Fact Type List.

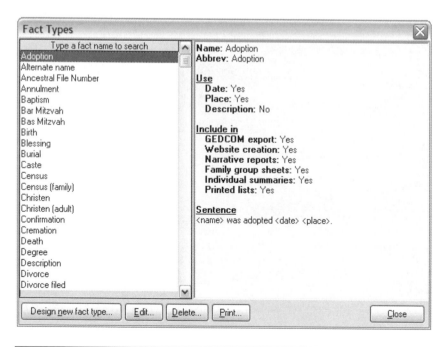

Creating a New Fact Type

To create a fact type that isn't already in the list, click the **"Design new fact type"** button. The following dialog will appear so you can tell RootsMagic whether the new fact type will be attached to people (like birth, death, etc), or to families (like marriage, divorce, etc).

RootsMagic will then display the following dialog so that you can enter the details for the new fact type you want to create.

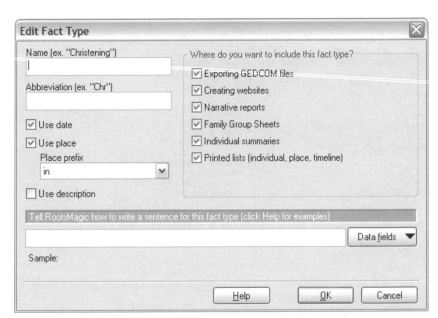

"Name" is where you enter the name for the new fact.

"Abbreviation" is where you enter a short version of the fact type name.

"Use date" lets you select whether your fact type needs a date. Although you might not think your fact needs this field, you might want to add it anyway. For example, a physical description might not be thought of as needing a date, but you might have facts stating that Aunt Peggy was a brunette from 1960 to 1985, but was a blonde from 1985 to 1987.

"Use place" lets you select whether your fact type needs a place. If you check this option, you need to select a "place prefix" which RootsMagic uses when writing sentences for this fact type. The place prefix is a word which goes in front of the place name, like "in New York". You will usually select "in" as the prefix, but some cases (like emigrated) you would use another prefix (like "from England").

"Use description" lets you select whether your fact type needs a description field. This is useful for fact types like Occupation or Religion where the fact has a value as well as a date and place.

"Where do you want to include this fact type?" lets you specify where RootsMagic uses your new fact. If you uncheck an item in this area RootsMagic will ignore the fact when performing that function. For example, if you uncheck **"Family Group Sheets"**, RootsMagic will not print that fact in family group sheets.

"Tell RootsMagic how to write a sentence for this fact type" is where you enter a "sentence template" to tell RootsMagic how you want this fact type to appear when printing books or creating websites. You simply write a sentence with "fields" to show where things like names, dates, and places fit.

For example, if you wanted the sentence for a birth fact to read like:

John Smith was born on 5 January 1900 in Avon, Polk County, Iowa.

Then you would write a sentence template like:

<name> was born <date> <place>.

When RootsMagic encounters a person's birth when writing a narrative report, it takes this template and replaces **<name>** with the person's name, **<date>** with the date of the birth, and **<place>** with the place of birth.

Sentence Template Fields	
Field	Description
<name>	RootsMagic replaces this with the person's name the first time it is used for a person. After it has been used once for a person, RootsMagic replaces it with "He" or "She".
<date>	RootsMagic replaces this with the fact date.
<place>	RootsMagic replaces this with the fact place.
<value>	RootsMagic replace this with the description field for the fact.
<avalue>	Works exactly like <value> except that RootsMagic adds a leading "a" or "an" in front of the description (ex. "a teacher" or "an engineer")
<hisher>	RootsMagic replaces this with "his" or "her"
<himher>	RootsMagic replaces this with "him" or "her"
<couple>	In family fact types, RootsMagic replaces this with the name of both the husband and wife (ex. "John Doe and Mary Smith") the first time it is used. After it has been used once for a couple, RootsMagic replaces it with "They".

Notice that when RootsMagic replaces **<date>** with the date, it adds the word "on" or "in" as appropriate, so you don't need to take that into account in your template. Also, when RootsMagic replaces **<place>** with the place, it adds the place prefix as defined above so that you don't have to add the word "in" or "from" or "to" to the sentence template. This ensures that the sentence will still read properly even if the date or place are blank for a particular fact.

Editing an Existing Fact Type

To edit an existing fact type, highlight the name of the fact you want to edit, and click on the **"Edit"** button. RootsMagic will display the "Edit Fact Type" dialog with the current settings for the fact. If you are editing one of RootsMagic's built-in fact types, some of the fields will be disabled so that you can't change them. Make any changes you want, then click the **"OK"** button to save the changes.

Deleting an Existing Fact Type

To delete a fact type from the fact list, simply highlight the fact name in the fact list, and click the **"Delete"** button. RootsMagic will ask if you really want to delete the fact type. You can only delete fact types that you have added yourself. RootsMagic won't let you delete any of the built-in fact types.

Searching for Information

Searching for needles in a haystack

Although you can move through your family on the Pedigree View or Family View, there are times when you need to find someone buried deep in your database.

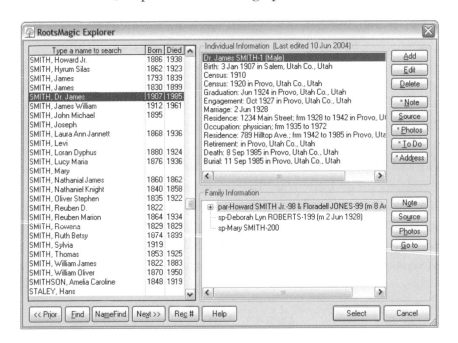

To find a person in your database, simply click the "Search" button on the toolbar and the RootsMagic Explorer will appear. You can also select **"Search, Person list"** from the main menu, or press **Ctrl+F** to bring up this screen.

The left side of the Explorer is an alphabetical list of every person in your database. You can use the up and down arrow keys to move the highlight bar from one name to another. The **PgUp, PgDn, Home** and **End** keys also move the highlight bar.

The right side of the Explorer displays information about the person highlighted in the left column. The top list displays all the facts (events) in the person's life, while the lower list displays the family (parents, siblings, spouses, and children) of the highlighted person. As you move the bar in the left column to different individuals, the information in the right side of the screen changes. When the person you are looking for is highlighted, click the **OK** button (or press **Enter**) to close the search screen and display the person on the main screen.

Finding a Person by Name

To find a person when you know their name, just begin typing the name in the Explorer, last name first. As you type the name, the highlight bar will move through the list to highlight the closest matching name. Just type the last name, then a comma, then begin typing the first name.

☺ Tip

When typing a name in the search screen, you can type a comma to finish out a surname. For example, if you are typing **"Christiansen, John"** and **"Ch"** has placed you on the first **"Christiansen"** in your database, just type a comma and RootsMagic will let you start typing the first name without typing the rest of the surname.

RootsMagic also includes a feature called NameFind. When you click the "NameFind" button RootsMagic will display a dialog where you can enter a given name and a surname.

When you fill in the name fields and click OK, RootsMagic will search for the first person that matches the name you enter. The nice thing is that it doesn't just search for the name entered in a person's edit screen. It will also search for married names as well. So if you search for Mary Smith, it will find Mary Ann Jones if she is married to William Smith.

Finding a Person by Other Information

To find a person (or group of people) when you don't know their name, click the **"Find"** button at the bottom of the RootsMagic Explorer and the "Search" dialog will appear.

Don't be intimidated by the search dialog. It simply wants you to tell it how to find a person. You tell it something about the person you are looking for, and RootsMagic will search through the entire database looking for someone that matches what you entered.

You can search just about any information for a person; names, dates, places, facts, sex, notes, and sources. When the search examines each person's information, it compares that information with whatever you enter in the "Search for?" field. You even get to select "how" it is compared.

Let's try an example. If you wanted to find everyone born in California, this is what you would do.

1) Click the drop arrow on the first field in the column titled "Field to search". A list of search fields will appear.
2) Select **"Birth place"** from the list.
3) We now need to tell RootsMagic what we want to look for in people's birth place. Since we want to find people whose birth place contains California, select **"contains"** from the list to the right of the button (the "Condition" list), and enter **"California"** in the "Search for" field to the right of that.
4) **That's it.** Just click the OK button and RootsMagic will move the highlight bar in the search screen to the first person whose birth place contains the text **"California"**. You can then click on the **"Next >>"** button to have RootsMagic find the next person who matches that criteria. The **"<< Prior"** button can be used to move back to the previous match that RootsMagic found.

Although we only completed one row in the "Search" dialog, RootsMagic provides 6 such rows, so your search can be as complex as you want. To the left of each criteria row is another list box where you can select between **"And"** and **"Or"**. This tells RootsMagic how to handle the multiple "criteria" rows. **"And"** means that RootsMagic must find each item to consider the person a match. **"Or"** means that RootsMagic should consider the person a match if any of the items match.

For example, if you entered these two lines of criteria:

Birth place contains Utah AND Death place contains Iowa

Then RootsMagic will only find people who were born in Utah AND died in Iowa. Both parts have to be true.

If you entered:

Birth place contains Utah OR Death place contains Iowa

then RootsMagic will find people who were born in Utah or people who died in Iowa. Only one part has to be true, although both can be.

In our example above, we used a "condition" of **contains**. Any time you select a field to search, RootsMagic provides a large number of ways to search the field. These "comparison" types depend on the type of field you select.

If search field is a...	You can compare in these ways...
Date	equal to, not equal to, is before, is after, is blank, is not blank, contains, does not contain
Place, Name, or Text	equal to, not equal to, contains, does not contain, less than, greater than, less than or equal, greater than or equal, sounds like, is blank, is not blank
Note	Contains, does not contain, is blank, is not blank
Source	Exists, does not exist, contains, does not contain, is blank, is not blank (for each part of the source or citation)

Editing From the Explorer

You may have noticed a lot of buttons on the RootsMagic Explorer. They let you edit just about any piece of information about the highlighted person.

➤ **Add** - Lets you add a new fact (event) to the highlighted person.
➤ **Edit** - Lets you edit the highlighted fact for the highlighted person. If the person's name is highlighted in the fact list, then RootsMagic will open the person's edit screen. This is especially useful when you need to edit a number of people and don't want to keep switching back and forth between the search screen and the main screen.

- ➤ **Delete** - Deletes the highlighted fact from the highlighted person. You will be asked to confirm that you really want to do this.
- ➤ **Note** - Lets you edit the note for the highlighted fact. If the person's name is highlighted in the fact list, then RootsMagic will let you edit the person's general note. An asterisk will appear on the button if the highlighted fact (or person) already has a note.
- ➤ **Source** - Lets you edit the sources for the highlighted fact. If the person's name is highlighted in the fact list, then RootsMagic will let you edit the person's general sources. An asterisk will appear on the button if the highlighted fact (or person) already has a source.
- ➤ **Photos** - Opens the scrapbook for the highlighted person. An asterisk will appear on the button if the person already has an item in their scrapbook.
- ➤ **ToDo** - Opens the to do list for the highlighted person. An asterisk will appear on the button if the person already has a to do item.
- ➤ **Address** - Opens the address dialog for the highlighted person. An asterisk will appear on the button if the person already has an address.
- ➤ **LDS** - Opens the LDS ordinance template for the highlighted person. This is only available if you have LDS support turned on for the database.
- ➤ **Go to** - Moves the selection in the Explorer to the person highlighted in the Family members list.
- ➤ There are also Note, Source, and Photos buttons to the right of the family list in the lower right corner. These work the same as the Note, Source and Photos buttons described above, except that they operate on the family notes, sources, and scrapbook.

Finding a Family

RootsMagic provides a family list that you can bring up by selecting **"Search, Family list"** from the main menu.

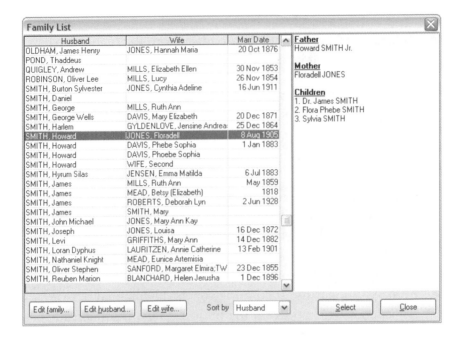

The family list will list the husband, wife, and the marriage date. As you move the highlight in the list from family to family, the right side of the screen will show the parents and children in the family. The data for the family list needs to be regenerated each time you select it, because RootsMagic does not store this data together normally.

You can sort the family list by the husband's name or by the wife's maiden name by selecting from the **"Sort by"** drop list.

You can search for individuals in the family list by typing the name of the husband or wife (depending on the sort order).

You can edit the family information by highlighting the family and clicking the "Edit family" button.

You can also edit the highlighted husband or wife by clicking on the "Edit husband" or "Edit wife" button.

If you click the **OK** button, RootsMagic will bring that couple up on the main screen.

Finding a Person's Relatives

To view all the immediate relatives of a person, select "View, View immediate family" from the main menu. RootsMagic will bring up a list of the immediate relatives of the highlighted person. This includes all parents, siblings, spouses, and children of the person.

If you want to see the immediate relatives of someone else in the list, you can highlight ther person and click the "Show family of highlighted person" button.

If you want to display one of these relatives on the main screen, you can either double click on the person's name, or highlight the person and click the "Select" button.

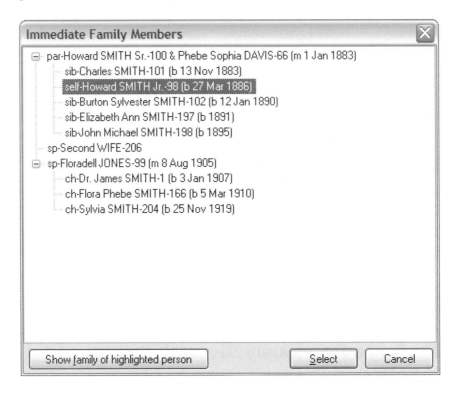

Bookmarking a Person

Often it is necessary to work with one person (or a small group of people) on a regular basis. RootsMagic makes it easy to bookmark and return to a person. Just highlight the person on the main screen, and do **"Search, Bookmarks"** from the main menu, or press **Ctrl+B**. The Bookmarks dialog will open.

If you want to add the person to the Bookmark list, click the "Bookmark current person" button.

Later, when you want to return to a bookmarked person, open the Bookmark dialog the same way, highlight the person in the Bookmark list, and click the "Go to selected person" button. You can also remove a bookmarked person by clicking the "Delete bookmark" button on this same screen.

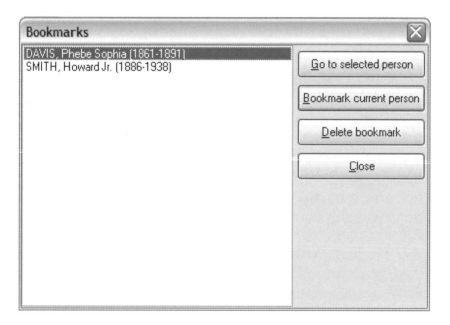

Finding a Previously Viewed Person

You may often find yourself wanting to return to a person you just recently viewed or worked on. RootsMagic maintains a "history list" of the most recently visited individuals in your database. Select "Search, History" from the menu to bring up the history list.

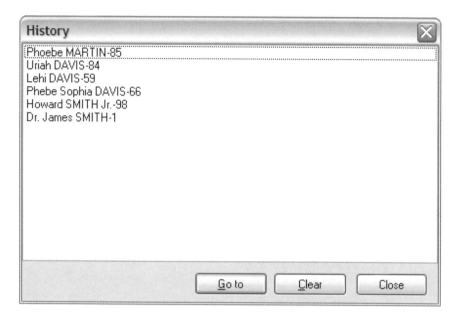

You can highlight any person in the history list and click the "Go to" button to return to that person on the main screen. RootsMagic also offers two commands to help navigate through the history list without actually bringing the list itself up.

> **Back** – "Search, Back" from the menu, or Ctrl + Left arrow will move back to the previously visited person on the main screen.
> **Forward** – If you have used the Back command, "Search, Forward" from the menu, or Ctrl + Right arrow will move forward again to the next visited person on the main screen.

Finding a Person on the Internet

RootsMagic provides an Internet Search to make it easy to hunt for your family. Highlight the person you want to search for on the main screen, then select "Search, Internet search" from the main menu.

RootsMagic will automatically fill out the given and surnames, but you can change them to whatever you want. Then select the site you want to search from the list, and click the "Begin searching" button. RootsMagic will open your browser and return the results of a search on that site for the name you entered.

RootsMagic also provides an IGI search feature to find information on the FamilySearch.org IGI site. This feature is described on page 253.

Notes – Telling Your Story

Anybody can make history. Only a great man can write it.
- Oscar Wilde

If names, dates and places are the bones of your family history, notes are the meat on those bones. **A note** is where you enter stories or more details about a person, family, or fact. For example, a birth note might include the name of the doctor that delivered the person, who witnessed the birth, how much the person weighed at birth, or other stories about the birth.

Where Can I Use Notes?

Notes can be associated with people, families, or facts in a person's life.

> **Individual notes** are tied to a person. These notes are where you enter information about a person that won't fit in one of the facts for the person. To enter or edit an individual note, open the person's edit screen and click the "Notes" tab. You can also highlight the person on the main screen and select "Edit, Notes, Person" from the main menu.

> **Family notes** are tied to a family. These notes are where you enter information about a family that you don't want to enter separately for the father, mother and children. To enter or edit a family note you can open the "Edit family" screen, and then click the "Notes" tab. You can also highlight the father or mother on the main screen and select "Edit, Notes, Family" from the main menu.

> **Fact notes** are tied to a fact in a person's life. These notes are where you enter more detailed information about the fact. To enter or edit a fact note you must first open the edit screen for the person by double clicking

your mouse on the person's name on the main screen. Then highlight the fact and click the **"Fact note"** button. You can also edit the fact note or sources by editing the fact and then clicking the **"Notes"** tab on the fact's edit screen.

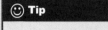 **Tip**

To quickly edit a fact note, just click your mouse in the note column of the fact list next to the desired fact.

And finally, you can edit any note from the Family Explorer by highlighting the desired person, family, or fact and clicking the "Note" button to the right of it.

Note Editor

When you edit a note, the note editor will appear. You can just begin typing in the note. The title bar of the note dialog will tell you what type of note you are entering, and who you are entering it for. In the dialog below, we are entering a "Birth" note for Dr. James Smith.

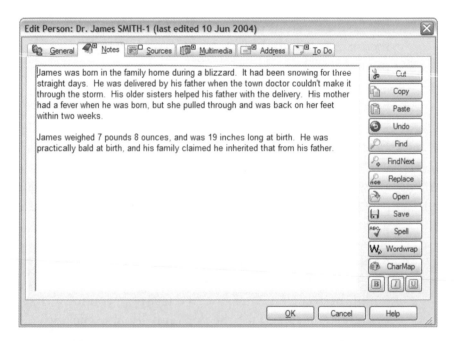

By clicking the buttons to the right of the editor, or clicking the right mouse button in the editor, you can access the edit commands.

Edit Command	Command Description	Hot Key
Cut	Places the marked text on the clipboard, then removes the marked text from the note.	Ctrl+X
Copy	Places the marked text on the clipboard.	Ctrl+C
Paste	Inserts any text from the clipboard to the note at the position of the blinking cursor.	Ctrl+V
Undo	Undoes the last editing command.	Ctrl+Z
Find	Lets you search for text within the note.	Ctrl+F
Find Next	Repeats the last search.	Ctrl+N
Replace	Lets you do a search and replace within the note.	Ctrl+H
Open	Read text into the note from a file.	Ctrl+O
Save	Save the note to a text file.	Ctrl+S
Spell check	Spell checks the current note. The spell checker is described in more detail in the chapter titled Tools (page 231).	F7
Word wrap	Word wraps the highlighted text. This is especially useful after importing a GEDCOM file that may have inserted hard returns into your notes.	Ctrl+W
Bold	**Bolds** the selected text.	Ctrl+B
Italics	*Italicizes* the selected text.	Ctrl+I
Underline	<u>Underlines</u> the selected text.	Ctrl+U
Character map	Opens the character map to let you select special (accented) characters.	Ctrl+T

If you want to change the font used in the note editor (to make it larger for example) do "Tools, Options, Main screen" from the menu and you can choose a new font. This font is only used for the data entry screen. The font for printing notes is selected in the separate report dialog screens.

When you are finished editing the note, click the OK button and RootsMagic will save the note and attach it to the appropriate person, family, or fact.

Private Notes

RootsMagic allows you to make parts of your notes private. Just place curly brackets { } around any text in the note that you want to be considered private.

When you print reports, export GEDCOM files, or create websites, RootsMagic will give you the option to include or ignore private notes. If you don't include private notes, RootsMagic will strip out everything between the curly brackets, including the brackets themselves.

If you do include private notes, you will also have the option whether to strip out the brackets when printing.

For example, if you have the following note:

This is a line of text.{ This is a private note.} This is another line of text.

choosing to ignore private notes would result in:

This is a line of text. This is another line of text.

Including private notes would result in either:

This is a line of text.{ This is a private note.} This is another line of text.

or

This is a line of text. This is a private note. This is another line of text.

depending on whether you chose to strip the brackets.

Sources – Proving It

Opinion has a significance proportioned to the sources that sustain it - Benjamin Cardozo

One of the most important things you can do when researching your family history is to document your information. Without proper documentation, the data you hand down to your descendants will probably have to be checked all over again.

Sources allow you to document where your information about a person, family, or fact came from. For example, a birth source might be a birth certificate, a baby announcement, or a family bible with details of the person's birth.

Where Can I Use Sources?

Sources can be associated with individuals, families, or facts in a person's life.

> **Individual sources** are tied to a person. These sources are where you enter information about a person that won't fit in one of the facts for the person. To enter or edit an individual source, open the person's edit screen and click the "Sources" tab. You can also highlight the person on the main screen and select "Edit, Sources, Person" from the main menu.

> **Family sources** are tied to a family. These sources are where you enter information about a family that you don't want to enter separately for the father, mother and children. To enter or edit a family source you can open the "Edit family" screen, and then click the "Sources" tab. You can also highlight the father or mother on the main screen and select "Edit, Sources, Family" from the main menu.

➤ **Fact sources** are tied to a fact in a person's life. These sources are where you enter more detailed information about the fact. To enter or edit a fact source you must first open the edit screen for the person by double clicking your mouse on the person's name on the main screen. Then highlight the fact and click the **"Fact source"** button. You can also edit the fact source or sources by editing the fact and then clicking the **"Sources"** tab on the fact's edit screen.

☺ **Tip**

To quickly edit a fact source, just click your mouse in the source column of the fact list next to the desired fact.

And finally, you can edit any source from the Family Explorer by highlighting the desired person, family, or fact and clicking the source button to the right of it.

Sources and Citations

To use sources to document your family, you need to understand the difference between a Source and a Citation.

A Source is the actual paper or document that provides information about your family. For example, a source might be a birth certificate, a book, or a tombstone. When you enter a source, you will enter information about the source, like a description, title, author, publisher, etc. You can also select a "Repository", which is just a fancy word for the place where the source is stored (like a library, courthouse, or even your own home).

A Citation is a reference to a source. By "citing" a source, you can allow a source to be entered just once, but cited many times. For example, if you cite a source that is a book, you only enter the details about the book once (title, author, publisher), but you can cite it as many times as you want. The citation can include details that are specific to that reference, such as the page number, volume, or film number.

When you click the "Source" tab for a person, fact or family, RootsMagic will display the source citation screen for that item. This screen is a list of all the sources that have been cited (referenced) for that item. For example, a birth source screen might look like the one below, with 3 sources being cited: a birth certificate, a baby announcement, and a journal entry.

To add a source citation you can either click the "Add new source" button, which lets you type in a new source (see page 80 for more details on adding sources), or the "Add existing source" button, which lets you select from a list of sources which have already been entered. This list of existing sources is known as the "Source list" and is described on page 79.

Once you have typed in a new source (described in the next section) or selected an existing source, RootsMagic will display the "Citation Details" dialog, where you can enter details about this use of the source.

As an example, if a person's birth were mentioned on page 93 of a book, you would cite the book as a source, and put "page 93" as the citation details. Citations for other people or facts might also cite the same source, but would likely have different details (page numbers). You can also enter actual text from the source, as well as any comments you have about this usage of the source.

RootsMagic also allows you to enter a "Citation quality" for the citation. You can specify the citation as being 1) of primary reliability, 2) of secondary reliability, 3) of questionable reliability, 4) unreliable, or 5) you can leave the quality blank. The reason the quality is assigned to the citation rather than the source is because a single source can have varying reliability depending on why it is cited. For example, a birth certificate might be a primary source for the person's birth, but only questionable (or even unreliable) when cited for the parent's birth date.

To edit a source, highlight the citation in the list and click the "Edit source" button. RootsMagic will bring up the Source dialog where you can make changes to the actual source. Be aware that any changes you make to the source here will also apply to any other citations using the same source.

To edit a citation, highlight the citation in the list and click the "Edit details" button. RootsMagic will bring up the Citation dialog where you can make any desired changes.

To delete a citation, highlight the citation in the list, and click the "Delete citation" button. RootsMagic will ask you to confirm that you want to delete the citation. Deleting the citation will not remove the source itself, just this reference to the source.

RootsMagic also offers "Memorize" and "Paste" commands, which will memorize the highlighted citation (including both source and citation details). You can then paste it into the citation list for other people, families, or facts.

The Source List

The heart of RootsMagic's source capabilities is the Source list. You can access the Source list by selecting "Lists, Source list" from the main menu.

The left side of the Source list is a list of all your sources. You can move through the list the same way you move through the individual search list. The right side of the screen displays information about the source highlighted in the left column. As you move the bar in the left column to a different source, the information in the right side of the screen changes.

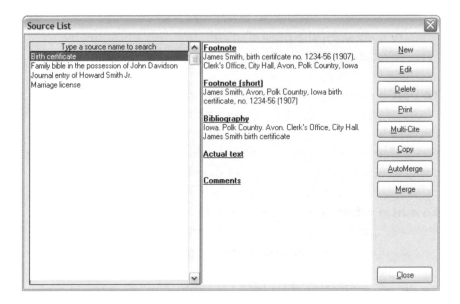

Adding a New Source

To add a new source, click the **"New"** button on the right side of
the Source Manager. RootsMagic will bring up a screen for you
to add the new source. Simply fill in the blanks for the source.

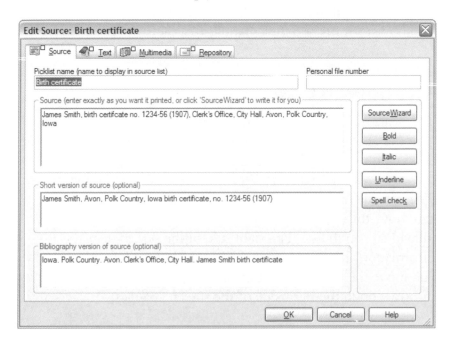

The **"Picklist name"** is the text you want displayed on the left side of the Source Manager for this source. This text does not print anywhere; it is only used in the list section of the Source list. Since RootsMagic sorts this list alphabetically, you can use the "Name" to make the source sort the way you want. For example, you could enter the names of census sources so that they group in an understandable fashion, like:

Census, Iowa, 1870
Census, Iowa, 1880
Census, Iowa, 1900
Census, New Mexico, 1910
Census, New Mexico, 1920
Census, Utah, 1910

The **"Personal file number"** field lets you tie your RootsMagic sources to your physical filing system. If you assign file numbers to the hard copies of your certificates, books, and other sources, you can enter that number here.

The **"Source"** field is where you will enter the source exactly as you want it printed as a footnote. You can enter the source in your own format, or in another accepted format like those in *Evidence!* by Elizabeth Shown Mills. You can use the "Bold", "Italic" and "Underline" buttons to format the source exactly the way you want. In addition, you can click the right mouse button for the same options that are available in the note editor (page 72), such as spell checking and the character map. RootsMagic can even help write the source for you. Just click the "SourceWizard" button to open the SourceWizard, which is described in the next section.

The **"Short version of source"** is an optional short version of the source which will print after the source has already been printed once in a report. If you don't enter a short version of the source, RootsMagic will use the main source field each time it is printed in the report.

The **"Bibliography version of source"** is an optional version of the source which will be used when RootsMagic is asked to print a bibliography for a report. If you don't enter a bibliography version of the source, RootsMagic will use the main source field each time it is printed in the report.

The **"Text"** tab of the source dialog lets you enter actual text from the source, and any comments about the source.

The "Actual text" is where you enter any text directly from the source. This isn't intended for you to enter the entire text of a book. It is useful for entering text such as tombstone inscriptions, obituaries, or even newspaper clippings. The "Comments" section lets you enter anything else you want regarding the source.

The **"Multimedia"** tab opens the multimedia scrapbook for the source so you can add scanned images of the source. Multimedia scrapbooks are described in more detail on page 89.

The **"Repository"** tab" lets you enter the address of the source, such as a library, courthouse, or in your own home. Repositories are described in more detail in the chapter titled "Repositories" on page 86.

The SourceWizard

When entering a source, you can have RootsMagic write the source for you by clicking the SourceWizard button.

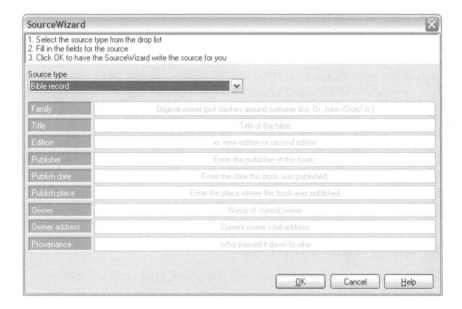

Select the desired source type from the "Source type" drop list in the SourceWizard. RootsMagic will display a set of fields for you to fill out for that source type. Hints and examples are displayed for each requested field.

In some places RootsMagic will ask you to enter a name with slashes around the surname. This helps the SourceWizard know how to handle the different ways names can appear in the source, short source, and bibliography.

Simply fill out each field and then click the OK button. RootsMagic will write the source, short version of the source, and bibliography version of the source for you. You can either accept the sources as written, or you can edit them to meet your own needs.

Editing a Source

To edit a source, highlight the name of the source in the Source list, then click the **"Edit"** button. RootsMagic will display the same dialog that you used when entering the source. Simply make the changes or additions you want and then click the **OK** button.

Deleting a Source

To delete a source, highlight the name of the source in the Source list, then click the **"Delete"** button. RootsMagic will ask if you really want to delete the source. If you select **"Yes"**, then RootsMagic will check if there are any people, families, or facts that cite the source. If there are, you will again be asked if you really want to delete the source. If you delete a source that has been cited, all the citations of that source will be deleted from the database as well. If you want to see which people, families, or facts are citing the source, you can use the Print command described below.

Printing Your Sources

If you want to find which people, families, and facts are citing a particular source, highlight the source in the Source Manager, then click the **"Print"** button. RootsMagic will print up the report dialog for the Source list (described on page 142).

Adding a Source to a Group of People

If you have a source that you need to add to more than one person, highlight the source in the Source list and click the "Multi-Cite" button. RootsMagic will bring up the selection screen (page 181) so that you can mark all the people you want to add the source to. RootsMagic will add the source to everyone you select.

Copying a Source

You may find a need to add a source that is very similar to another source already entered in the source list. In this case you can highlight the similar source in the source list and click the Copy button. RootsMagic will make an exact copy of the source which you can edit. The new source will have the same name as the original source except with (copy) added to the end of the name.

Merging Duplicate Sources

There may be times when you find multiple copies of the same source in the Source Manager. This sometimes happens when importing a GEDCOM file that came from a program that doesn't allow you to reuse sources.

RootsMagic offers two options for merging duplicate sources.

1. To merge all exact duplicate sources into a single source open the source list ("Lists, Source list" from the menu) and click the AutoMerge button. RootsMagic will merge all the exact duplicate sources in your database. If there is any difference in the source footnote, short footnote, bibliography, actual text or comments field, the sources will not be merged.
2. To merge two sources (even if one is a little different from the other), highlight the primary source in the source list and click the "Merge" button. The "Merge" button will change to "Select dup". You can then highlight the duplicate source in the source list and click the "Select dup" button. RootsMagic will ask if you want to merge the duplicate source into the primary source. RootsMagic does not combine the text from the two sources. It only keeps the text from the primary source and merges citations of the duplicate source into the primary source.

Repositories – Where Is It?

Now where did I find that source?

Almost as important as documenting where you found your information, is where that information is located. These locations, whether they be libraries, archives, courthouses, or even your own home, are called "repositories".

The Repository Page

When adding or editing a source, you can click the "Repository" tab where RootsMagic lets you enter both a primary and a secondary repository for the source. You can also enter the **"Call number"** within the repository where the source can be found.

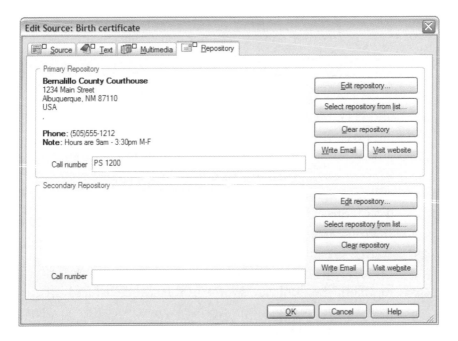

To enter (or edit) a repository, click the "Edit repository" button to the right of the repository area. RootsMagic will open an entry screen where you can add the name, address, phone number, fax, email and website of the repository. You can also add notes about the repository like directions, business hours or names of employees you need to work with.

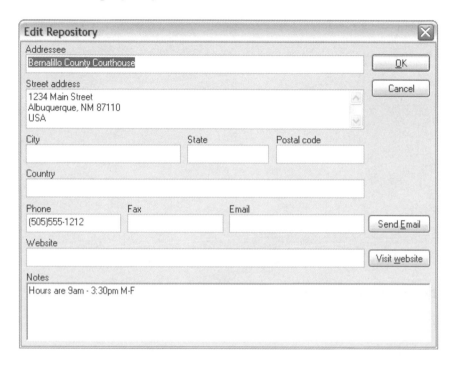

The "Send Email" and "Visit website" buttons make it quick to send an email or visit the website of the repository.

When you have filled in the blanks, click the OK button and RootsMagic will return to the source's repository page.

If the source is in a repository that you have already entered, click the "Select repository from list" button, and RootsMagic will open the Repository list, described in the next section. You can choose the repository from the list.

The Repository List

The Repository list is simply a list of places, such as libraries, archives, courthouses, fellow researchers; or any place that a source might be found **To access the Repository list**, select "Lists, Repository list" from the main menu.

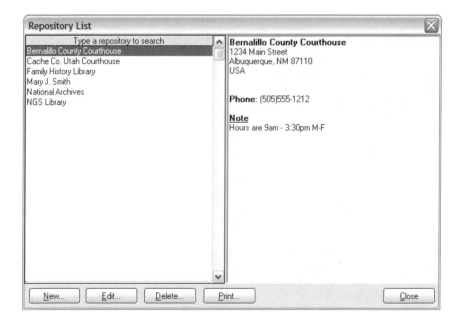

To add a new repository click the "Add" button, and enter the repository as described in the previous section.

To edit a repository, highlight the name of the repository in the list, then click the "Edit" button. RootsMagic will display the same dialog that you used when entering the repository. Simply make the changes or additions you want, then click the OK button.

To delete a repository, highlight the name of the repository in the list, then click the "Delete" button. RootsMagic will ask if you really want to delete the repository. If you delete a repository that has a source, to do task, or correspondence referencing it, the source, task, or correspondence will have their repository or contact field cleared.

To print a list of all information associated with a repository, highlight the repository and click the "Print" button. RootsMagic will open the report dialog for you to print the repository list for that repository (see page 141 for more details).

Pictures, Sound, and Video

One picture is worth a thousand words. —Fred R. Barnard

As computers become more powerful, and the cost of scanners and digital cameras come down, it becomes easier to add photos to your computerized genealogy. RootsMagic provides a Multimedia Scrapbook for each person, family, fact, source and place in your database. This scrapbook can hold scanned photos, files, sound clips, and video clips.

To add a photo or other media item to a person, family, fact, source, or place, click the "Multimedia" tab on the edit screen for the item.

You can also add photos to a person or family by highlighting the person (or parent of the family) on the main screen and click your mouse on the "Photos" button on the toolbar. Then select either **"Person scrapbook"** or **"Family scrapbook"** from the popup menu.

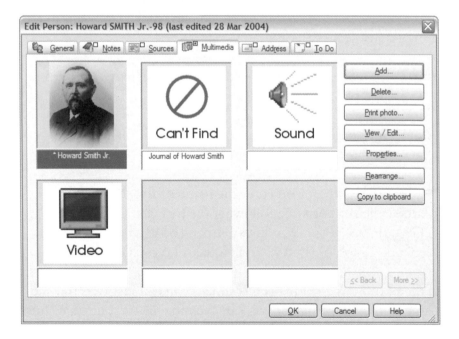

Adding a Scrapbook Item

To add a photo to the scrapbook, click the "**Add**" button on the multimedia screen. The following screen will appear.

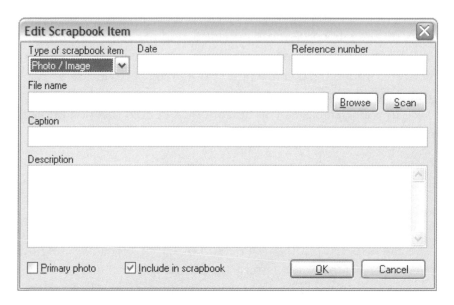

"Type of scrapbook item" lets you select whether you want to add a photo, file, sound clip, or video clip. Since you want to add a photo, just leave "Photograph" selected.

"Date" lets you enter a date for the scrapbook item. This can be the date the photo was taken.

"Reference number" lets you enter a personal file number which ties this record to your own filing system.

"Filename" is where you enter the name of the scanned photo. RootsMagic supports the following file formats: PCX, Targa (TGA), JPEG (JPG), Windows Bitmap (BMP), Portable Network Graphics (PNG), and Kodak Photo CD (PCD).

If the photo has already been scanned, you can just type the name of the image file, or you can click the "**Browse**" button to find the scanned image using the Windows file dialog.

If the photo hasn't been scanned yet, and you have a scanner attached to your computer, just click the "Scan" button, and RootsMagic will run your scanner's software for you. When the scanner software is finished, RootsMagic will ask you to save the scanned photo. Just enter a filename and image file type, and RootsMagic will do the rest.

"Caption" allows you to enter a one line description of the photo, like "John on his first birthday".

"Description of scrapbook item" allows you to enter a more detailed description of the photo. This is especially useful for listing the names of all the people in a family photograph.

"Primary photo" lets you tell RootsMagic which photo in a scrapbook is the one that you want printed on charts, since RootsMagic allows you to add unlimited photos to a scrapbook. The primary photo has an asterisk in front of the caption in the scrapbook page, and is also displayed on the main screen for the person.

"Include in scrapbook" lets you tell RootsMagic whether you want this photo to be included when you print the scrapbook.

Once you have everything entered the way you want, click the OK button and RootsMagic will add the photo to the scrapbook.

If you ever want to change the caption, description, or other settings for the photo, simply click on the photo in the scrapbook, then click on the "Properties" button at the top of the scrapbook. RootsMagic will open up the same dialog you used when adding the photo, and you can make the changes desired.

To bring a photo into RootsMagic, you need to "scan" the photo using a scanner. A scanner scans the photo (much like a copy machine) and then saves that scanned image in a graphics file. If you don't have a scanner yourself, you may have a friend or relative who does. If not, there are many copy centers that offer scanning services. You can take your photos in and leave with a disk of scanned images that can be used in RootsMagic and other programs.

For some great tips on scanning, you can visit the website at: **http://www.scantips.com**.

Adding a document, sound clip or video clip to a person's scrapbook works exactly the same way as adding a photo, except that the **"Scan"** button is not available, nor are the **"Primary photo"** or **"Include in scrapbook"** checkboxes.

Warning

RootsMagic only stores links to multimedia items, not the items themselves. Therefore, moving the items to another directory will cause RootsMagic to lose track of them and report the links as invalid.

If this happens, you can use RootsMagic's search and replace feature (page 233) to change the pathnames of the linked multimedia items.

Removing a Scrapbook Item

To remove an item (photo, document, sound or video clip) from the scrapbook, click your mouse on the item in the scrapbook screen, then click the **"Delete"** button. RootsMagic will ask if you really want to remove the item. Click on **"Yes"** to remove the item.

When RootsMagic removes an item from the scrapbook, it simply removes the link to the item. It doesn't actually remove the image, document, sound or video file from the hard drive itself.

Rearranging Scrapbook Photos

Since you may not always add your photos in the same order you want them displayed or printed in the scrapbook, RootsMagic allows you to rearrange them any way you want (for example, from baby picture to 100th birthday photo). Just click the "Rearrange" button on the scrapbook, and RootsMagic will bring up a list of all photos in the current scrapbook, which you can drag and drop into the desired order.

Copying Photos to the Clipboard

If you ever need to use a copy of a photograph in another program, you can click your mouse on the photo in a person's scrapbook, then click the "Copy to clipboard" button. RootsMagic will copy the selected photo to the clipboard so it can be pasted into other programs.

Editing Scrapbook Photos

When the scrapbook screen is displayed, the photos displayed are "thumbnails" of the actual photo. A thumbnail is a small, low-resolution copy of the image that is designed to display fast on the screen.

To edit the photo, click your mouse on the photo you want to see, then click the "View / Edit" button. You can also just double click your mouse on the photo in the scrapbook.

Although RootsMagic isn't (and doesn't claim to be) a graphics editing program, it does allow you to perform some editing of your photos. Simply make any desired changes, then close the editor, and RootsMagic will ask if you want to save the modified photo.

The "View" menu in the Photo Editor provides options for viewing the photo. You can view it full (actual) size, or you can have RootsMagic fit it to the editor window. If you select full size, and the image is too large for the window, scroll bars will appear for your use. You can also zoom the photo in and out from this menu.

The "Image" menu allows you to manipulate the photo. You can flip or rotate the photo. You can also "crop" (or trim) the photo.

To crop a photo, first click the "Select rectangle" button on the toolbar, then use the mouse to select the rectangular area you want to keep (by clicking, dragging, and releasing). If you mess up, just click once outside the rectangle and try again. Once you have the rectangle where you want it, click the Crop button on the toolbar, or select "Crop" from the Image menu.

The "Color" menu lets you adjust characteristics of the image. You can adjust the brightness, contrast, hue, saturation, and gamma of the image. Simply select one of the options from the Color menu, and adjust the scroll bar on the dialog that appears. The preview photo will change to show what the image will look like if you press OK. To accept the changes, press OK. To cancel without making any changes, press Cancel.

Printing Scrapbook Photos

RootsMagic allows you to print your photos in a variety of ways.

If you simply want to print a single photo, open the scrapbook, click on the photo you want to print, then click the "Print photo" button.

If you want to print your photo with data, just choose any of the RootsMagic printouts that offer a checkbox to include photos, and make sure that box is checked. RootsMagic will print photos in books, individual summary, family group sheet, scrapbooks, or photo tree).

Viewing and Editing a File

When you add a file to a scrapbook, RootsMagic displays an image of a document in the scrapbook. **To view or edit a file**, click your mouse on the image, then click on the "View / Edit" button. You can also double click your mouse on the image. RootsMagic will open the file using the program which is associated with that file type in Windows Explorer.

Playing Sound and Video Clips

When you add a sound clip or video clip to a scrapbook, RootsMagic displays a picture of a speaker or monitor in the scrapbook. **To play a sound or video clip**, click your mouse on one of these pictures, then click on the **"View / Edit"** button. You can also double click your mouse on the speaker or monitor picture.

Getting Details on Your Scrapbook Items

If you ever need to find out where all your scrapbook items (photos, sound and video clips) are located on your hard disk, you can print the "Multimedia List" which is available under the "Lists" section of the "Reports" dialog.

Putting Your Family on Paper

There is no such thing as a paperless world.

One of the main reasons a person buys a genealogy program is to print out their family on paper. Not surprisingly, everybody wants his or her family displayed in a different format.

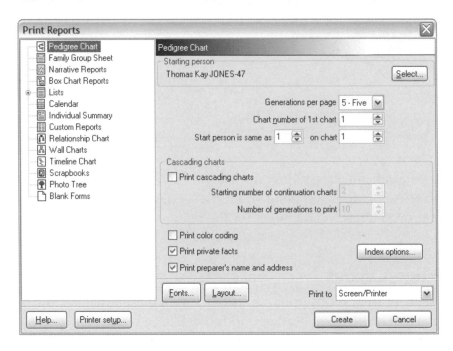

To print a report in RootsMagic, click on the printer button on the toolbar, or select **"File, Print"** from the main menu. You can also select individual report types from the **"Reports"** item of the main menu. The **"Print Reports"** dialog that appears has a list of report types down the left side of the screen.

You can click your mouse on any of the report types to set the options for that report. When you have the report type and options selected, just click the **"Create"** button at the bottom of the dialog to generate the printout.

Report Options

While each type of report will have its own options, most report types will use some or all of the following options. Rather than repeatedly discuss these options for each and every report, we'll mention them here.

Selecting the Fonts for the Report

"Fonts" lets you select the fonts that RootsMagic will use for the selected report.

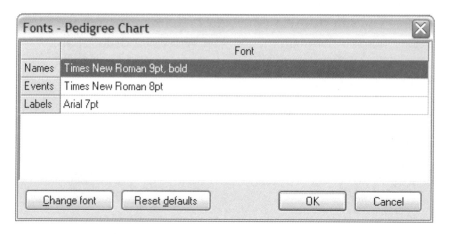

You can highlight a font in the list and click the "Change font" button to select the font and point size to be used. The "Reset defaults" button will reset all the fonts for the report back to their original settings.

Page Layout

Many of the various printout dialogs have a button that lets you change the margins, headers and footers, page orientation and starting page number for the selected report type. For example, if you change the page layout for group sheets, it doesn't affect the page layout of pedigree charts. Clicking the "Layout" button on the report dialog will open the following dialog.

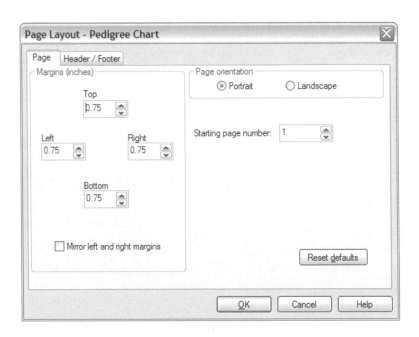

Margins allows you to enter the top, bottom, left and right margins for the printout. There is also a check box where you can tell RootsMagic to mirror (switch) the left and right margins. This is useful when you are going to print a report double sided on the paper, and want a larger margin for binding the report into a book.

Orientation lets you tell RootsMagic which direction to print on the paper. Portrait prints the standard way on the page, while landscape prints "sideways" on the page.

Starting page number allows you to number your printout starting with a page number other than 1. This is useful when you are printing multiple reports, and want to bind them together into a single book.

Reset defaults is a button which simply restores RootsMagic's defaults for the current page layout.

To change the header or footer for the report, click the Header/Footer tab in the Page Layout dialog.

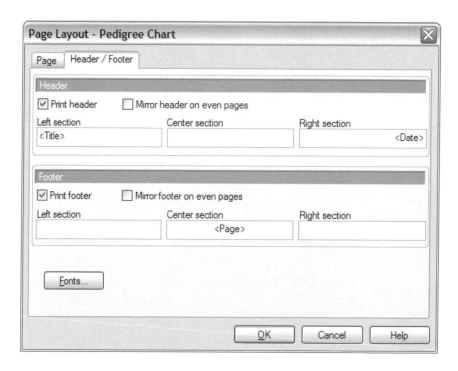

Check the "Print header" box if you want RootsMagic to print a header at the top of each page. The header will consist of the text entered in the **"Left section"**, **"Center section"**, and **"Right section"** along with a separator line. These "sections" tell RootsMagic where to print the text within the header. For example, anything entered in the "Center section" will be centered in the header. You can also select different fonts for each section by clicking the "Fonts" button.

You can enter text into any section, or special "codes" that RootsMagic will convert when printing. These codes are:

\<Date\>   RootsMagic will replace this with the current date.

\<Page\>   RootsMagic will replace this with the current page number.

\<Title\>   RootsMagic will replace this with a title designed specially for this printout.

\<File\>   RootsMagic will replace this with the name of the database.

You can also swap the left and right header sections (mirror header) on even pages. This is useful for example when you are printing double sided and want the header to be a mirror image on facing pages.

The footer works exactly the same way as the header, except that it is printed at the bottom of each page.

Selecting the Print Destination

The **"Print to?"** drop list lets you select the destination for the printout. You will usually select **"Screen/Printer"** so that you can preview the printout on the screen, then print the report if you want. You can also print many of the reports to a file using the **"Rich Text File (*.rtf)"**, **"Ascii Text File (*.txt)"**, or "Acrobat file (*.pdf)" options.

If you send your printout to the Screen/Printer, RootsMagic will display it in the print preview window.

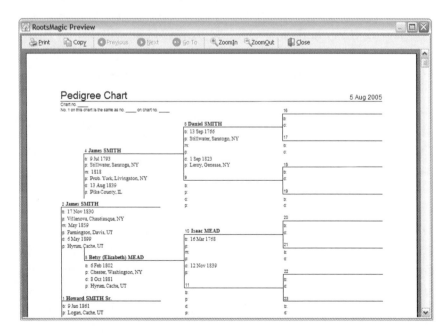

➢ Clicking the **"Print"** button will print the displayed document. You will be given the choice of:

➤ Printing the entire document, the currently displayed page, or a range of pages.

➤ Selecting how many copies to print

➤ Selecting whether to print only the odd or even pages. This is useful when you want to print double sided. You can print all the odd pages first, then reload those pages reversed into the printer, and then print the even pages.

➤ Clicking the **"Copy"** button will cause RootsMagic to copy the currently displayed page to the clipboard in Enhanced Meta File (EMF) format. You can then go into Word or many other programs and paste the page into that program.

➤ Clicking the **"Previous"** button will display the previous page of the document. If there is no previous page, this button will be disabled.

➤ Clicking the **"Next"** button will display the next page of the document. If there is no next page, this button will be disabled.

➤ Clicking the **"GoTo"** button will let you go to the first or last page of the document, or to any page number in the document. If you select the "Page" option, just enter the page number and click OK and RootsMagic will display that page.

➤ Clicking the **"Zoom In"** button will cause RootsMagic to zoom in on the document, so you can see more detail.

➤ Clicking the **"Zoom Out"** button will cause RootsMagic to zoom out of the document, so you can see more of the document on screen at once.

➤ Clicking the **"Close"** button will exit from the print preview and return back to the main screen.

If you send your printout to a Rich Text File (*.rtf) file, RootsMagic will ask you for a file name, and will then save the printout in Rich Text format. It will then automatically open the file in your word processor. You can turn this auto open feature off in the program options. RTF is a text format that preserves the formatting of the file, such as fonts, tabs, indents, superscripts, etc. Most current word processors can read RTF files, so this is a good way to get a RootsMagic report into your word processor for extra editing.

If you send your printout to an Ascii Text File (*.txt), RootsMagic will ask you for a file name, and will then save the printout to a text file. It will then automatically open the file in your text editor. This text file will retain the text itself, but will lose most formatting. This format can be useful if you want to send a report to somebody by electronic mail (email).

If you send your printout to an Acrobat file (*.pdf), RootsMagic will ask you for a file name, and will then save the printout to an Adobe Acrobat file. It will then automatically open the file in the Acrobat reader (if you have it installed on your system). If you don't have it, you can download it for free from:

http://www.adobe.com

Pedigree Charts

The pedigree chart is a visual display of the direct ancestors of the person on the far left of the chart. It is one of the most commonly used charts in genealogy.

Pedigree Chart   5 Aug 2005

Chart no.
No. 1 on this chart is the same as no. _____ on chart no. _____

```
                                                                        16 James SMITH
                                                                           b: 9 Jul 1793
                                            8 James SMITH                  d: 13 Aug 1839
                                              b: 17 Nov 1830
                                              p: Villenova, Chautauque, NY 17 Betsy (Elizabeth) MEAD
                                              m: May 1859                     b: 6 Feb 1802
            4 Howard SMITH Sr.                p: Farmington, Davis, UT        d: 8 Oct 1881
              b: 9 Jun 1861                   d: 8 May 1899
              p: Logan, Cache, UT             p: Hyrum, Cache, UT          18 Henry William MILLS
              m: 1 Jan 1883                                                   b: 1 May 1807
              p: Hyrum, Cache, UT           9 Ruth Ann MILLS                  d: 9 Oct 1885
              d: 6 Apr 1936                   b: 30 Mar 1834
              p: Hyrum, Cache, UT            p: Quincy, Adams, IL           19 Elmira POND
 2 Howard SMITH Jr.                           d: 31 Dec 1910                  b: 14 Feb 1811
   b: 27 Mar 1886                             p: Hyrum, Cache, UT             d: 3 Sep 1904
   p: Hyrum, Cache, UT                                                     20 Uriah DAVIS
   m: 8 Aug 1905                                                              b: 5 May 1805
   p: Logan, Cache, UT             10 Lehi DAVIS                              d: 18 Oct 1863
   d: 9 Feb 1938                      b: 28 Oct 1832
   p: Garland, Box Elder, UT         p: Fountain Co., IN                   21 Phoebe MARTIN
                                     m: 6 Jun 1852                            b: 7 May 1806
            5 Phebe Sophia DAVIS     p:                                       d: 6 Feb 1905
              b: 22 Dec 1861         d: 18 Mar 1899
              p: Three Mile Creek, Box Elder  p: Basin City, Big Horn, WY 22 Charles BARNUM
              d: 1 Mar 1891                                                   b:
              p: Hyrum, Cache, UT          11 Eliza BARNUM                    d:
                                             b: 15 Oct 1837
                                             p: Mt. Morris, Levengston, NY 23 Elizabeth THORNE
                                             d: 11 Feb 1911                   b:
                                             p: Hyrum, Cache, UT             d:
 1 James SMITH                                                            24 Samuel William JONES
   b: 3 Jan 1907                                                             b: 18 Jun 1828
   p: Salem, Utah Co., Utah         12 Thomas William JONES                  d: 5 Jun 1910
   m: 2 Jun 1928                       b: 11 Apr 1848
   p:                                  p: Pembroke Dock, Pembrokeshire, So. Wales 25 Eleanor BAINBRIDGE
   d: 8 Sep 1985                       m: 21 Mar 1868                         b: 29 May 1832
   p: Provo, Utah Co., Utah           p: Salt Lake City, Salt Lake, UT       d: 2 May 1902
                                      d: 12 Nov 1912
 sp: Deborah Lyn ROBERTS             p: Paradise, Cache, UT                26 John KAY
            6 Thomas Kay JONES                                                b: Aug 1819
              b: 3 Apr 1869                                                   d: 2 Sep 1884
              p: Paradise, Cache, UT      13 Margaret Chatterley KAY
              m: 11 Jul 1885                 b: 1 Nov 1848                  27 Sarah CHATTERLEY
              p:                             p: Pilkington, Lancashire, England  b: 5 Aug 1818
              d: 4 May 1930                  d: 30 Sep 1924                   d: 9 Apr 1884
              p: Paradise, Cache, UT         p: Paradise, Cache, UT
 3 Floradell JONES                                                        28 William GRIFFITHS
   b: 4 Dec 1888
   p: Paradise, Cache, UT
   d: 14 N...
```

To generate a pedigree chart for a person, highlight the start person on the main screen, then click the Print button on the toolbar, then click **"Pedigree Chart"** on the report list.

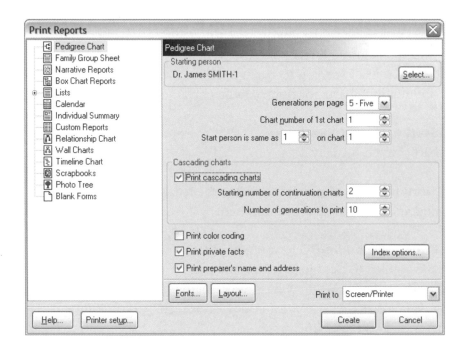

"Starting person" is the person who the pedigree chart will begin with. You can click the "Select" button to change this person.

"Generations per page" lets you print 4, 5, or 6 generations of ancestors on each page of the printout.

"Chart number of 1st chart" is the number of the first chart printed (usually 1).

"Start person is same as X on chart Y" lets you specify whether the starting person is already on a chart you have previously printed. These are usually both 1.

"Cascading charts" makes RootsMagic create a series of pedigree charts that span more generations than will fit on a single page. RootsMagic will still use the generations per page selected, but will print additional pages as necessary and number the pages. Each person in the farthest right generation of a chart will become person number 1 on subsequent charts.

If you select cascading charts, the following options become available. Although you should usually just use the default values, RootsMagic allows you to change them in case you need to print continuation charts for ones you have printed previously.

"Start # of continuation charts" is the number of the second chart printed (usually 2).

"Total number of generations" is the total number of generations for all charts combined.

"Print color coding" lets you print any color coding you may have applied to people in your database. If you mark this checkbox, RootsMagic will print the name of each person in the same color as they are color coded on screen. Color coding is described on page 226.

"Print private facts" lets you choose whether RootsMagic should include any facts (birth, marriage, or death) that you have marked as "private".

"Index options" lets you choose whether RootsMagic should print an index of everyone in the pedigree charts, along with options for the index. This is useful mainly when printing cascading charts, which have more than a single page.

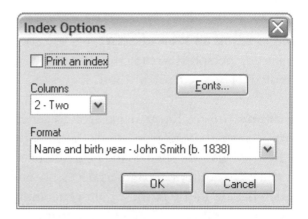

> "Print an index" lets you choose whether an index should be printed.
> "Columns" lets you choose how many columns the index should contain.
> "Format" lets you choose how to print each name in the index. You can choose name only, or the name with the birth year, or the name with the birth and death year.

Family Group Sheets

The Family Group Sheet is probably the most heavily used printout in genealogy. It is essentially a table that lists all of the facts for a father, mother, and children in a family.

Family Group Sheet — 5 Aug 2005

Husband	Thomas William JONES	
Birth	11 Apr 1848	Pembroke Dock, Pembrokeshire, So. Wales
Death	12 Nov 1912	Paradise, Cache, UT
Burial	15 Nov 1912	Paradise, Cache, UT
Marriage	21 Mar 1868	Salt Lake City, Salt Lake, UT
Father	Samuel William JONES (1828-1910)	
Mother	Eleanor BAINBRIDGE (1832-1902)	
Wife	**Margaret Chatterley KAY**	
Birth	1 Nov 1848	Pilkington, Lancashire, England
Death	30 Sep 1924	Paradise, Cache, UT
Burial	3 Oct 1924	Paradise, Cache, UT
Father	John KAY (1819-1884)	
Mother	Sarah CHATTERLEY (1818-1884)	
Children		
1 M	**Thomas Kay JONES**	
Birth	3 Apr 1869	Paradise, Cache, UT
Death	4 May 1930	Paradise, Cache, UT
Burial	7 May 1930	Paradise, Cache, UT
Spouse	Myra GRIFFITHS (1868-1951)	
Marriage	11 Jul 1885	
2 M	**John Kay JONES**	
Birth	4 Feb 1872	Paradise Cache Ut
Death	23 May 1914	
Burial		
Spouse	Jane BRADLEY (-)	
Marriage	12 May 1892	
3 M	**Samuel Kay JONES**	
Birth	27 Mar 1873	Paradise, Cache, UT
Death	17 Mar 1943	Paradise, Cache, UT
Burial		Paradise, Cache, UT
Spouse	Ann HOWELLS (1870-1913)	
Marriage	19 Sep 1898	
4 F	**Margaret Kay JONES**	
Birth	1 Jul 1875	Paradise Cache Ut
Death	21 Jun 1878	
Burial		
Marriage		

To generate a family group sheet, highlight the father or mother of the family on the main screen, then click the Print button on the toolbar, then click **"Family Group Sheet"** in the report list.

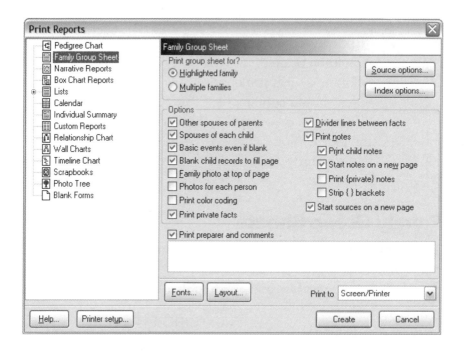

"Print group sheet for" lets you decide if you want to print a single group sheet for the current family, or if you want to print a bunch of group sheets all at once. If you pick the second option, RootsMagic will bring up a list of every person in your database when you click the **"Create"** button. This selection screen is described in the chapter titled "Custom Reports" (page 181), and allows you to select the families you want to print group sheets for.

"Other spouses of parents" lets you specify whether RootsMagic should print other spouses of the parents on the group sheet.

"Spouses of each child" lets you specify whether RootsMagic should print spouses of each child on the group sheet.

"Basic events even if blank" determines whether RootsMagic will print birth, marriage, death and burial facts for each person even if they are blank. If this box is unchecked, RootsMagic will only print facts that have been entered for the person. If a person doesn't have a death fact entered, RootsMagic will not print a blank one for them.

☺ **Tip**

It is possible to turn off certain facts from ever printing in the family group sheet. Select **"Lists, Fact type list"** from the main menu and a list of every fact type will appear. Double click on the fact you want to turn off. You can then uncheck the "Family Group Sheet" checkbox for that fact and RootsMagic will not print that fact on any group sheets.

"Blank child records to fill page" specifies whether RootsMagic will print enough child records to fill the entire page (even if they are blank). For example, if you print a group sheet for a family with two children, the group sheet might only use the top half of the page, unless you check this box.

"Family photo at top of page" tells RootsMagic whether to print a family photo above the group sheet. You need to add a photo to the family's scrapbook before RootsMagic can print it.

"Photos for each person" tells RootsMagic whether to print individual photos for each person on the right side of the group sheet. In order to line photos up nicely, RootsMagic will print a blank box for people who do not have a photo entered.

"Print color coding" lets you print any color coding you may have applied to people in your database. If you mark this checkbox, RootsMagic will print the name of each person in the same color as they are color coded on screen. Color coding is described on page 226.

"Print private facts" lets you choose whether RootsMagic should include any facts (birth, marriage, death, etc.) that you have marked as "private".

"Print divider lines between events" tells RootsMagic whether to draw horizontal lines between each event on the group sheet.

"Print notes" determines whether RootsMagic will print any notes with the group sheet. If this box is checked, RootsMagic will print all the family, individual, and fact notes associated with the family. You can select whether the notes will begin on a separate page following the group sheet, or whether they will immediately follow the last child on the group sheet. Remember that if you ask RootsMagic to print notes immediately after the last child, you should uncheck the "Print blank child records to fill page", or the notes will start on a new page anyways. You can also disable printing of the children's notes, in case you are printing multiple group sheets and don't want to duplicate the children's notes on multiple group sheets.

"Print private notes" and **"Strip brackets"** let you choose whether RootsMagic should print any private notes you have entered. Private notes are described in more detail on page 74.

"Comments" allows you to enter text that will be printed at the bottom of the family group sheet. Marking the "Print preparer and comments section" box will enable this feature.

"Start sources on new page" tells RootsMagic whether to start printing the sources on a new page.

The "Sources" button lets you tell RootsMagic how to print sources for the group sheet (if at all). It will bring up the following dialog.

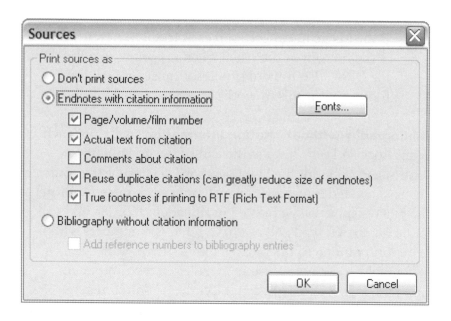

"Don't print sources" means just what it says… your sources won't be printed.

"Endnotes with citation information" tells RootsMagic to print the sources at the end of the report. The first time the source is encountered it will be printed in full. The second and subsequent times the source is encountered (within the same document), RootsMagic will print the "short" version of the source if you have entered it (otherwise it will print the full source again). You can choose several options along with this choice.

> **"Page/volume/film number"** tells RootsMagic to print the page number field from the citation details after the source.

> **"Actual text from citation"** tells RootsMagic to print the actual text from the citation after the source.

> **"Comments about citation"** tells RootsMagic to print the comments about the citation following the source.

> **"Reuse duplicate citations"** causes RootsMagic to not print exact duplicate sources over and over. If RootsMagic encounters a citation that it has already printed, it will reference the already printed source again.

➢ **"True footnotes if printing to RTF"** will cause RootsMagic to export sources as true footnotes (printing at the bottom of the page) when exporting to a Rich Text file (*.rtf). Your word processor must support true footnotes for this to work.

"Bibliography without citation information" will print each source once and only once at the end of the document. RootsMagic will print the "bibliography" version of the source if you have entered it (otherwise it will print the source footnote). The bibliography will be printed in alphabetical order, and will not be numbered (and will not have reference numbers within the report pointing to the bibliography). If you want the bibliography to be numbered (and have reference numbers within the report text), you can select the "Add reference numbers to bibliography entries" checkbox.

"Index options" lets you choose whether to print an index for the group sheet(s). This is the same option as described on page 106.

Narrative Reports

Narrative reports allow you to print a family history of a person. The narrative report can include the ancestors of the person (parents, grandparents, etc) or the descendants (children, grandchildren, etc).

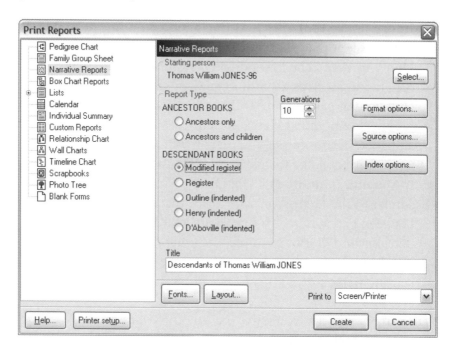

"Starting person" is the person whom the report will begin with. You can click the "Select" button to change this person.

"Report type" lets you select what type of book you want to print.

➢ **Ancestors only** - Prints a narrative history of the starting person and his/her ancestors. Only direct ancestors are included in the book.

➢ **Ancestors and children** - Same as the ancestor book, except that children of each ancestor are also included.

➢ **Modified Register** - Prints a narrative history of the starting person and his/her descendants. The book is broken into chapters by generation.

- ➢ **Register** - Prints a narrative history of the starting person and his/her descendants. The book is broken into chapters by generation.
- ➢ **Outline (indented)** - Prints a narrative history of the starting person and his/her descendants grouped by family. Many non-genealogists find this book format easier to follow. Each generation is indented from the previous generation, and is numbered in an outline format (I, A, 1, i, a, etc).
- ➢ **Henry (indented)** - Same as the indented outline descendant book, except that the numbering system follows the Modified Henry format. The first person is number 1, and each generation receives an additional digit stating the order of that child in that generation. If there are more than 9 children in a family, the modified Henry system uses the letters of the alphabet. For example, the person with Henry number 1.b.3 is the third child of the eleventh child of the starting person.
- ➢ **D'Aboville (indented)** - The D'Aboville numbering format is similar to the Henry format, except that a period is added between generations, so that digits instead of letters can be used beyond 9. For example, the person with D'Aboville number 1.11.3 is the third child of the eleventh child of the starting person.

"Title of report" lets you enter the title for your report. RootsMagic will provide a default title that you can change if you want.

"Number of generations to print" lets you specify how many generations you want to include in your report.

The **"Format Options"** button will display a dialog with a number of options for customizing your narrative report.

- ■ **"Include notes"** specifies whether RootsMagic will include notes in the report. If notes are included, RootsMagic will insert them in the text. For example, a birth note would immediately follow the sentence about the person's birth date and place.

- **"Print private notes"** and **"Strip brackets"** let you choose whether RootsMagic should print any private notes you have entered. Private notes are described in more detail on page 74.
- **"Print private facts"** lets you choose whether RootsMagic should include any facts (birth, marriage, death, etc.) that you have marked as "private".
- **"Include photos"** specifies whether RootsMagic will include photos of individuals in the report. RootsMagic will use the primary photo for the person as entered in their multimedia scrapbook. You can also choose the size RootsMagic should print the photos. Photos are not included when printing to a text file.
- **"Date format in report"** lets you select how RootsMagic will print dates in the report. Month names can be abbreviated or fully spelled out.
- **"Start each generation on a new page"** specifies whether RootsMagic will start each new generation (chapter) on a new page.
- **"Print preparer's name and address"** lets you specify whether RootsMagic should print the preparer's name and address at the bottom of the printout. You can set the preparer's name and address in the options screen (page 264).
- **"Print uplines"** is only available when printing Modified Register or Register reports. This option will print a list of ancestors (and generations) following the name of each descendant in the report. For example:

John Doe (David-3, Samuel-2, William-1) was born in 1820.

- **"Print color coding"** lets you print any color coding you may have applied to people in your database. If you mark this checkbox, RootsMagic will print the name of each person in the same color as they are color coded on screen. Color coding is described on page 226.

- **Sentence template for people with no entered facts**
lets you tell RootsMagic what to write for people with no
facts. When creating the narrative report, RootsMagic
will write sentences for each fact entered for a person. If
a person has no facts, then RootsMagic can't normally
write anything about the person. If you don't want
anything written about the person, then you can leave this
field blank. Some suggestions for this template are:

<name> was born.

<name> was born (date unknown).

No further information is known about <name>.

Source options lets you tell RootsMagic how to print sources
for the book (if at all). It will bring up the source print option
dialog described on page 110.

"Index options" lets you choose whether to print an index for
the report. This is the same option as described on page 106.

☺ **Tip**

When printing a report to a Rich Text (RTF) file
RootsMagic will not actually build the index at the end of
the report (since RootsMagic has no way of knowing how
your word processor will paginate the report). Instead,
RootsMagic will "mark" each person in the RTF file so
that your word processor can build the index itself. This
is extremely useful in case you want to add more text,
photos, or make other changes.

For example, to build the index in Microsoft Word after
you have imported the RTF file, move to the end of the
file, then select **"Insert, Index and Tables"** from Word's main
menu. Select whatever options you want, then click OK
and Word will generate the index for you. WordPerfect
users can generate an index in a similar manner.

Box Chart Reports

Box chart reports let you print ancestor or descendant box charts which can be used in books because they print on standard size pages. They can also be selected when publishing your information using the RootsMagic Publisher described later.

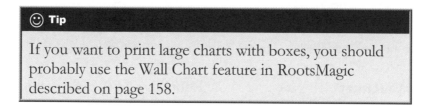

☺ **Tip**

If you want to print large charts with boxes, you should probably use the Wall Chart feature in RootsMagic described on page 158.

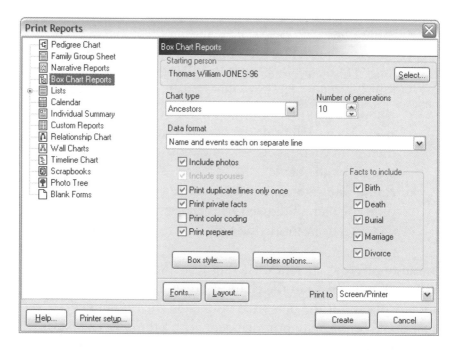

"Starting person" is the person who the report will begin with. You can click the "Select" button to change this person.

"Chart type" lets you select what type of chart you want to print.

➢ **Ancestors** - Prints a box chart of the starting person and his/her ancestors. Only direct ancestors are included in the chart.

➢ **Descendants** - Prints a box chart of the starting person and his/her descendants. Each generation is indented a bit to the right, and connecting lines are drawn to show the links between generations.

"Number of generations" lets you specify how many generations you want to include in your box chart.

"Data format" lets you select how RootsMagic will print each person's information in the chart. You can choose from:

➢ **Single line** – RootsMagic will print the name of each person followed by their birth and death date on the same line. This is intended to be a compact format and no boxes are drawn around the single line for each person.

➢ **Name and events each on a separate line** – RootsMagic will print the name of each person on a line, then print each fact type you choose to print on a separate line under the name.

➢ **Name and events word wrapped** – RootsMagic will print the name followed by the facts you choose word wrapped to fit inside the box.

"Include photos" specifies whether RootsMagic will include photos of individuals in the chart. RootsMagic will use the primary photo for the person as entered in their multimedia scrapbook. Photos are not included when printing to a text or Rich Text file.

"Include spouses" lets you choose whether spouses should be included in the descendant box chart. This option is not applicable when printing an ancestor chart.

"Print duplicate lines only once" lets you choose whether to print duplicate lines every time they are encountered, or whether to only print duplicate lines the first time they are encountered. Duplicate lines will generally occur when you have cousin marriages.

"Print private facts" lets you choose whether RootsMagic should include any facts (birth, marriage, etc.) that you have marked as "private".

"Print color coding" lets you print any color coding you may have applied to people in your database. If you mark this checkbox, RootsMagic will color a person's box in the same color as they are color coded on screen. The boxes of non color coded people will be printed in the color chosen in the "Box style" dialog. Color coding is described on page 226.

"Print preparer" lets you specify whether RootsMagic should print the preparer's name and address at the bottom of the printout. You can set the preparer's name and address in the options screen (page 264).

"Box style" lets you select the style of the border which RootsMagic draws around each person. When you click the "Box style" button, the following dialog box will appear. From this dialog, you can choose what style you want, whether you want the box to have a shadow, and what color the box and shadow should be.

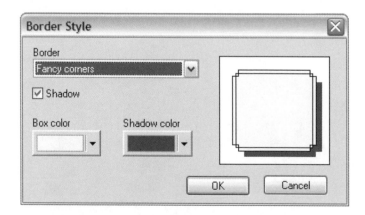

Just play with the various settings and see what the box will look like. Pick a style you like then click the OK button. If you decide you don't want to change the box style after all, you can click the Cancel button and RootsMagic won't modify the box style.

"Index options" lets you choose whether to print an index for the box chart. This is the same option as described on page 106.

"Facts to include" lets you choose which facts you want to include in each person's box. You can choose from birth, death, burial, marriage, and divorce.

Lists

RootsMagic provides a large assortment of printable lists from the report dialog. Just highlight the list type and RootsMagic will display an option dialog specific to the list you want to print.

All lists offer the ability to print to the screen or printer, a text file, or a Rich Text file. You can also select the font for each list.

Address Labels

RootsMagic will print mailing labels using any number of standard Avery labels.

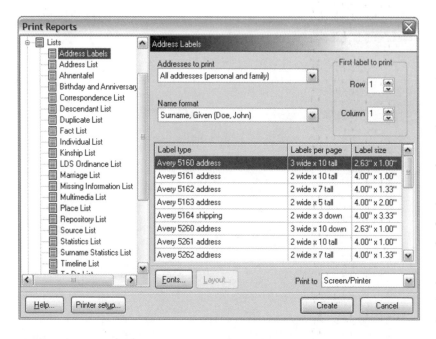

"Addresses to print" lets you decide which people you want to include in the list. If you pick "Select individuals", RootsMagic will bring up a list of every person in your database when you click the **"OK"** button. This selection screen is described in the chapter titled "Custom Reports" (page 181), and allows you to select the people you want to print labels for.

"Name format" specifies how RootsMagic will print the names on the labels. The first two choices will cause RootsMagic to print the address list using the actual names entered for the person in the database. The third choice will cause RootsMagic to use the name (or names) that you entered in the person's address dialog box.

"First label to print" is especially useful when you have a partially printed label sheet, and need to start printing your labels somewhere in the middle of the sheet.

"Label type" lets you select what type (and size) label you want to print on. Just highlight the desired label type.

Address List

The address list allows you to print any or all of the addresses that you have entered for people using the **"Edit, Address"** command.

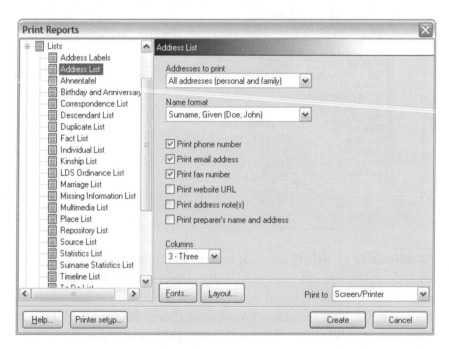

"Addresses to print" lets you decide which people you want to include in the list. If you check "Select individuals", RootsMagic will bring up a list of every person in your database when you click the **"OK"** button. This selection screen is described in the chapter titled "Custom Reports" (page 181), and allows you to select the people you want in your list.

"Name format" specifies how RootsMagic will print the names in the address list. The first two choices will cause RootsMagic to print the address list using the actual names entered for the person in the database. The third choice will cause RootsMagic to use the name (or names) that you entered in the person's address dialog box.

"Print preparer's name and address" lets you specify whether RootsMagic should print the preparer's name and address at the bottom of the printout. You can set the preparer's name and address in the options screen (page 264).

The remaining checkboxes let you tell RootsMagic which additional address information (phone number, fax, etc) you want to print for each person.

In addition to the normal print destinations, RootsMagic will also let you save the address list to a comma delimited text file that can be used by most word processors, databases, and other programs.

"Columns" lets you choose how many columns to print the address list in.

Ahnentafel

The Ahnentafel (which means "Ancestor Table" in German) is an ancestor report. The Ahnentafel is in narrative form, and each individual in the report is assigned an "Ahnentafel number." This numbering system makes it easy to determine a person's parents. The Ahnentafel number of a person's father is exactly twice the person's number and the mother's number is twice the person's number plus one.

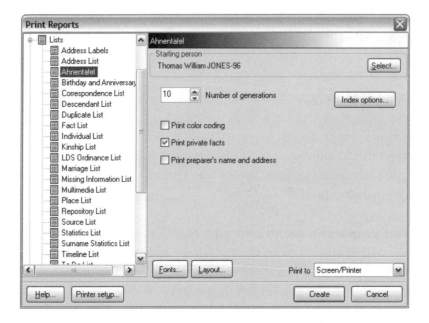

"Starting person" is the person who the report will begin with. You can click the "Select" button to change this person.

"Number of generations" lets you specify how many generations you want to include in your report.

"Print color coding" lets you print any color coding you may have applied to people in your database. If you mark this checkbox, RootsMagic will print the name of each person in the same color as they are color coded on screen. Color coding is described on page 226.

"Print private facts" lets you choose whether RootsMagic should include any facts (birth, marriage, death, etc.) that you have marked as "private".

"Print preparer's name and address" lets you specify whether RootsMagic should print the preparer's name and address at the bottom of the printout. You can set the preparer's name and address in the options screen (page 264).

"Index options" lets you choose whether to print an index for the report. This is the same option as described on page 106.

Birthday and Anniversary List

The birthday and anniversary list prints birthdays and / or anniversaries sorted by date. You can choose to include everyone in your database, or just selected individuals. If you choose "Selected individuals", RootsMagic will bring up a list of every person in your database when you click the **"OK"** button. This selection screen is described in the chapter titled "Custom Reports" (page 181), and allows you to select the people you want in your list.

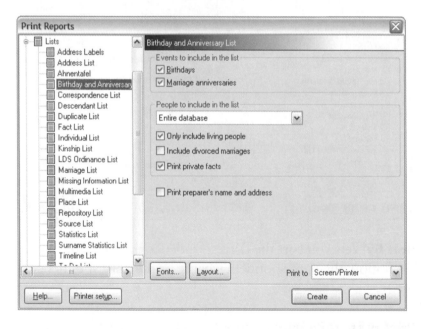

You also have several options which can be used to filter out individuals, such as only including living people and including (or ignoring) marriages with divorces entered. You can also have RootsMagic print the preparer's name and address at the end of the list. You can set the preparer's name and address in the options screen (page 264).

Correspondence List

The correspondence log is a list of all correspondence you have entered using the **"Lists, Correspondence list"** command.

You can select which types of correspondence you want to print (mail, phone, email, fax, other, sent or received. You can even have RootsMagic print the full address of each correspondent.

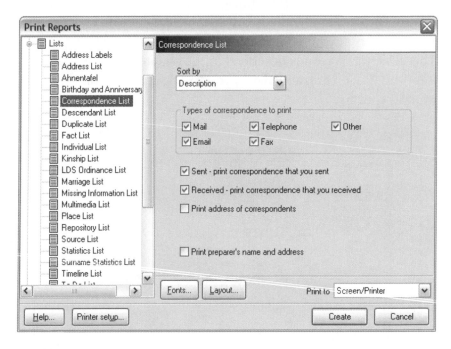

"Sort by" lets you sort the correspondence by either the description, the correspondent's name or the correspondence date.

"Print preparer's name and address" lets you specify whether RootsMagic should print the preparer's name and address at the bottom of the printout. You can set the preparer's name and address in the options screen (page 264).

Descendant List

The descendant list is an indented list of the highlighted person and his or her descendants (children, grandchildren, etc). Each person is printed on a single line and each generation is indented to the right of the previous generation. You can print this list with either one line per person, or full birth, marriage and death information on multiple lines.

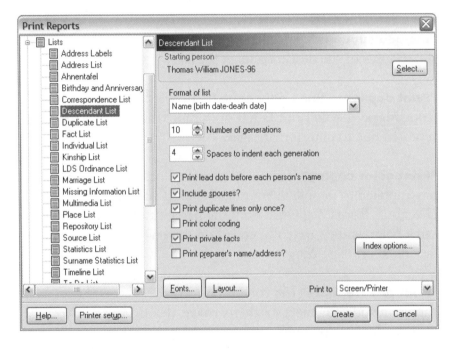

"Starting person" is the person who the report will begin with. You can click the "Select" button to change this person.

"Format of list" lets you print each person on a single line (with just their birth and death date), or print up to 4 lines for each person (name, birth date and place, marriage date and place, and death date and place). You can also choose to print the name, birth dates and death dates in columns.

"Number of generations" lets you specify how many generations you want to include in your list.

"Spaces to indent each generation" lets you specify how much each generation will be indented to the right. If you make this number small, you can fit more generations across the page. If you make this number larger, you can spread the list across the page more.

"Print lead dots before each person's name" tells RootsMagic whether it should print a string of dots before each person's name in the list. This can sometimes make the list easier to read.

"Include spouses?" specifies whether RootsMagic should print the spouses of the descendants in the list.

"Print duplicate lines only once?" specifies whether RootsMagic should print family lines more than once if they are repeated due to cousin marriages.

"Print color coding" lets you print any color coding you may have applied to people in your database. If you mark this checkbox, RootsMagic will print the name of each person in the same color as they are color coded on screen. Color coding is described on page 226.

"Print private facts" lets you choose whether RootsMagic should include any facts (birth, marriage, death, etc.) that you have marked as "private".

"Print preparer's name and address" lets you specify whether RootsMagic should print the preparer's name and address at the bottom of the printout. You can set the preparer's name and address in the options screen (page 264).

"Index options" lets you choose whether to print an index for the report. This is the same option as described on page 106.

Duplicate Record List

The duplicate record list is a report of possible duplicate records in your database. The list will contain pairs of records that might be duplicates. This report is particularly useful when you want to merge individual records and want a list of records that need merging.

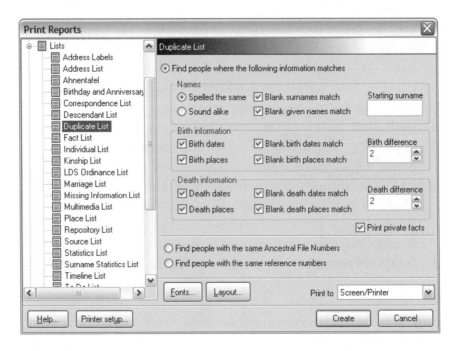

RootsMagic offers three different kinds of duplicate searches.

Find people where the following information matches lets you set options to have RootsMagic compare people using.

➢ **Names** lets you tell RootsMagic how people's names must match to be considered duplicates. You can specify whether matching names have to match exactly, or if they just need to sound alike. You can also choose whether blank names (both given and surnames) will be considered as matches with non blank names. Checking these boxes often leads to many false duplicates.

- ➤ **Starting surname** lets you tell RootsMagic where in the database to start the duplicate search. If you leave this blank, then RootsMagic will search the entire database for duplicates. If you enter "D", then RootsMagic will start with surnames beginning with the letter "D". If you enter "Jones", then RootsMagic will start with people with the last name "Jones".
- ➤ **Birth information** tells RootsMagic whether to compare birth information of people when checking for duplicates. You can choose to compare birth dates and / or birth places. You can also enter a maximum number of years between birth dates. If you set this value to 0, RootsMagic will only consider two individuals duplicates if they were born the exact same year. A value of 5 means that two individual's birth dates can be 5 years apart and still be considered duplicates. The smaller this number, the fewer duplicates RootsMagic will find. You can also tell RootsMagic whether you want to consider individuals without birth dates or birth places as possible duplicates. If you don't check these boxes, RootsMagic will not consider any individuals whose birth date (or place) is blank, even if they match in other ways.
- ➤ **Death information** works the same as the birth options (except with death data of course).

Print private facts lets you choose whether RootsMagic should include any facts (birth, marriage, death, etc.) that you have marked as "private".

Find people with the same Ancestral File Numbers finds individuals with matching Ancestral File numbers. All other criteria is ignored.

Find people with the same reference numbers finds individuals with matching Reference numbers (REFN). All other criteria is ignored.

Fact List

The Fact List is one of the most useful printouts available in RootsMagic. It allows you to print lists of people associated with any fact in your database (including any user-defined facts you have created).

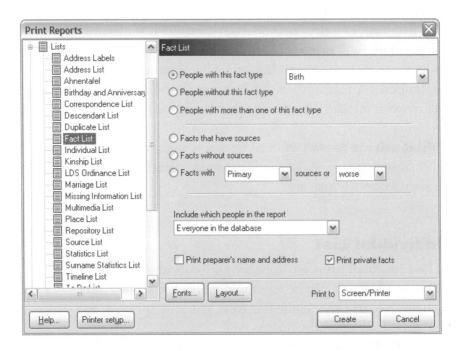

You can print a list of people who have or don't have a specific fact. Simply select the desired fact type from the drop list, and you can print a list of everyone with that fact, everyone without that fact, or everyone with more than one of that fact. For example, if you wanted a list of everyone in your database that you have not entered a birth for, select birth from the list, select "People without this fact type", and click Create.

You can also print a list of facts that have or don't have sources. You can even print facts that have sources of a certain quality. For example, if you want a list of facts that have solid documentation, you might print a list of "Facts with Primary sources or Better".

"Print preparer's name and address" lets you specify whether RootsMagic should print the preparer's name and address at the bottom of the printout. You can set the preparer's name and address in the options screen (page 264).

"Include which people in the report" lets you decide which people you want to include in the list. You can print everyone in the database, or select people from a list. If you check "Selected" RootsMagic will bring up a list of every person in your database when you click the **"Create"** button. This selection screen is described in the chapter titled "Custom Reports" (page 181), and allows you to select the people you want in your list.

"Print private facts" lets you choose whether RootsMagic should include any facts (birth, marriage, death, etc.) that you have marked as "private".

Individual List

The Individual list is an alphabetical list of any or all people in your database. It can be as simple as just the names of the individuals, or can include the facts, parents, spouses, and children for each individual as well.

"People to print" lets you decide which people you want to include in the list. You can print everyone in the database, or select people from a list. If you check "Selected" RootsMagic will bring up a list of every person in your database when you click the **"Create"** button. This selection screen is described in the chapter titled "Custom Reports" (page 181), and allows you to select the people you want in your list.

You can also print several specialized lists, including people who have no parents entered in the database, people who have more than one set of parents entered in the database, and people who aren't linked to anyone else in the database (no spouses, children, or parents).

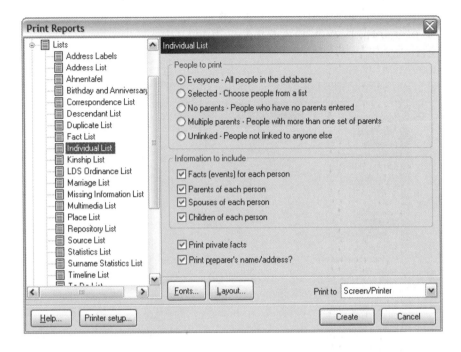

"Information to include" specifies what information you want printed for each person in the list, including facts for each person, or the parents, spouses, or children of each person.

"Print private facts" lets you choose whether RootsMagic should include any facts (birth, marriage, death, etc.) that you have marked as "private".

"Print preparer's name and address" lets you specify whether RootsMagic should print the preparer's name and address at the bottom of the printout. You can set the preparer's name and address in the options screen (page 264).

Kinship List

One of the coolest lists in RootsMagic is the Kinship list. RootsMagic will print a list of every person in the database that is related to the highlighted person, and will display the relationship to that person. It will include all degrees of ancestors, descendants, siblings, aunts, uncles, and cousins (including how many times removed). It will even get spouses of your relatives. Be prepared though, if you have a big database, this list can get pretty long!

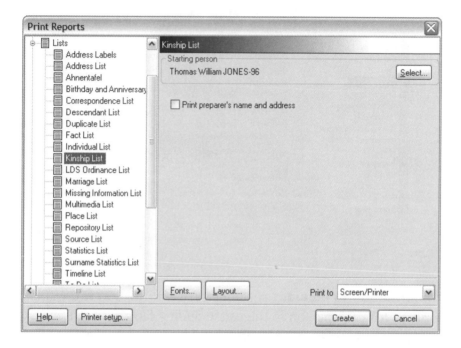

"Starting person" is the person RootsMagic will find relatives for. You can click the "Select" button to change this person.

"Print preparer's name and address" lets you specify whether RootsMagic should print the preparer's name and address at the bottom of the printout. You can set the preparer's name and address in the options screen (page 264).

LDS Ordinance List

The LDS ordinance list (there are actually two of them) will print LDS ordinance information for the people in your database.

"Report type" lets you select which ordinance list to print.

➢ **Individual ordinances** - lists individuals and the dates for LDS baptism, endowment, and sealing to parents.

➤ **Marriage sealings** - lists families and the marriage date and sealing to spouse date.

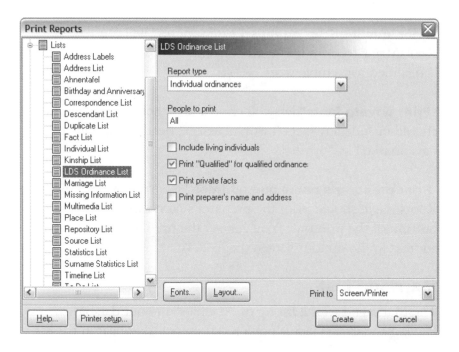

"People to print" lets you select which individuals to include in the selected list.

➤ **All** – prints everyone in the database
➤ **Only those missing ordinances** - prints only individuals who are missing at least one ordinance
➤ **Only those with all ordinances completed** - prints only individuals who are not missing any ordinances
➤ **Only those with "submitted" ordinances** - prints only individuals who have at least one ordinance with a status of "Submitted".
➤ **Only those with "qualified" ordinances** - prints only individuals who have at least one ordinance which is qualified for temple work.

"Include living individuals" gives you the option to ignore living individuals (since you can't do temple work for them anyways).

"Print 'qualified' for qualified ordinances" will cause RootsMagic to print the word "qualified" for any ordinance that is qualified for temple work.

"Print private facts" lets you choose whether RootsMagic should include any facts (birth, marriage, death, etc.) that you have marked as "private".

"Print preparer's name and address" lets you specify whether RootsMagic should print the preparer's name and address at the bottom of the printout. You can set the preparer's name and address in the options screen (page 264).

Marriage List

The Marriage List is a listing of "couples" in your database. Having a marriage fact is not a requirement to appear in the list.

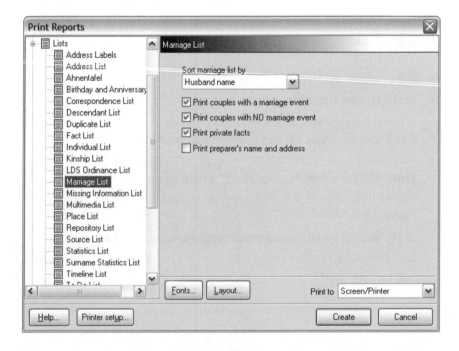

"Sort marriage list by" lets you sort the marriage list by the husband's surname, the wife's surname, the marriage date, or the marriage place.

You can have RootsMagic print couples with a marriage event, or those without a marriage event, or both.

"Print private facts" lets you choose whether RootsMagic should include any facts (birth, death, etc.) that you have marked as "private".

"Print preparer's name and address" lets you specify whether RootsMagic should print the preparer's name and address at the bottom of the printout. You can set the preparer's name and address in the options screen (page 264).

Missing Information List

The Missing Information List creates a list of individuals missing any fact(s) or part of a fact that you choose. You can select multiple fact types in a single report.

Click and highlight as many facts as you want RootsMagic to check for each person. Then select what part of the fact needs to be missing.

➤ **Are missing this fact** will print a person if any of the highlighted facts are missing for the person.
➤ **Have this fact but date is blank** will print a person if the fact exists, but the date is missing.
➤ **Have this fact but place is blank** will print a person if the fact exists, but the date is missing.

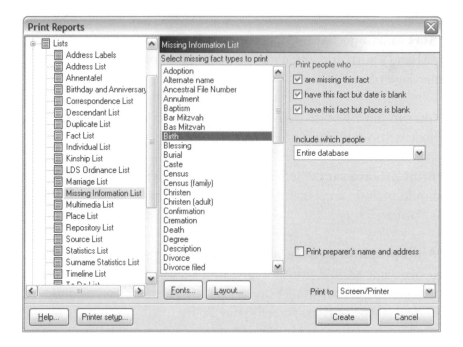

"Include which people" lets you decide which people you want to include in the list. If you check "Select individuals", will bring up a screen for you to select the people you want to include. This selection screen is described in the chapter titled "Custom Reports" (page 181), and allows you to select the people you want in your list.

"Print preparer's name and address" lets you specify whether RootsMagic should print the preparer's name and address at the bottom of the printout. You can set the preparer's name and address in the options screen (page 264).

Multimedia List

Since the RootsMagic scrapbook links to multimedia items on your hard disk, it is possible to lose track of which photos, video and sound clips you are linking to. The multimedia list generates a printout of multimedia items your database is using, including the full path name and what the item is linked to.

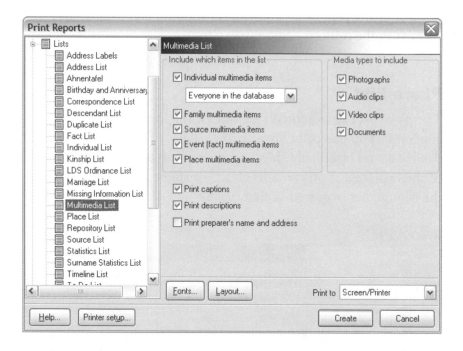

"Include which items in the list" lets you decide which multimedia items you want to include in the list. You can select any combination of multimedia items connected to people, families, sources, events, or places. If you choose Individual multimedia items, you can futher choose whether to include everyone or just selected people. If you choose "Selected people", RootsMagic will bring up a list of every person in your database when you click the **"Create"** button. This selection screen is described in the chapter titled "Custom Reports" (page 181), and allows you to select the people you want in your list.

You can further filter the list by choosing whether to include any combination of photos, audio clips, video clips, or documents.

You also have the option to print the caption and description for each multimedia item as well.

"Print preparer's name and address" lets you specify whether RootsMagic should print the preparer's name and address at the bottom of the printout. You can set the preparer's name and address in the options screen (page 264).

Place List

The place list can potentially be one of the longest reports you generate. You can print an alphabetical list of every place in your database, and optionally show every event that happened in each of those places. You can also choose a single place along with all the events that occurred in that place.

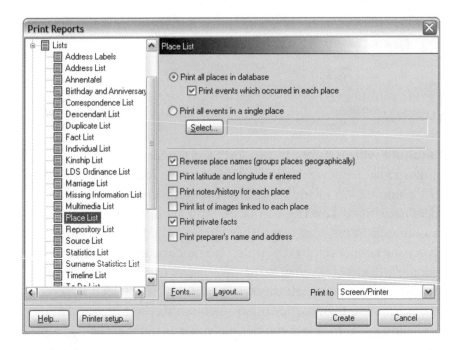

When places are printed, RootsMagic can reverse them so that the general part of the place name is first to sort places geographically. For example, if you mark the checkbox to reverse place names, places will be listed like:

New Mexico, Bernalillo Co., Albuquerque
New Mexico, Santa Fe Co., Santa Fe
Utah, Salt Lake Co., Draper
Utah, Salt Lake Co., Salt Lake City
Utah, Utah Co., Orem
Utah, Utah Co., Provo

"Print latitude and longitude if entered" will cause RootsMagic to print the latitude and longitude for each place that you have entered that information.

"Print notes/history for each place" causes RootsMagic to print any notes you entered for the place. You can also have RootsMagic print a list of any images the each place's multimedia scrapbook.

"Print private facts" lets you choose whether RootsMagic should include any facts (birth, death, etc.) that you have marked as "private".

"Print preparer's name and address" lets you specify whether RootsMagic should print the preparer's name and address at the bottom of the printout. You can set the preparer's name and address in the options screen (page 264).

Repository List

The repository list will print either a single repository (libraries, archives, etc) or all repositories in the database. You can also have RootsMagic include all the sources, to-do tasks, and correspondence for each repository. This is especially useful if you want to print a list of things you need to do at a repository.

"Address" tells RootsMagic to print the full address for each repository.

"Note" tells RootsMagic to print any notes you have entered for each repository.

"Sources in repository" will print all sources which reside in each repository. Additionally you can include the actual text and comments about each source.

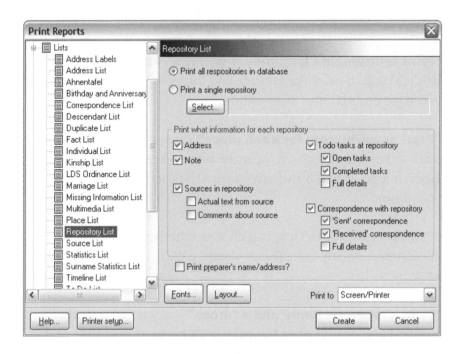

"Todo tasks at repository" will print all to-do tasks for each repository. You can choose whether to print open or completed tasks (or both), and can ask RootsMagic to print the full details for each todo task.

"Correspondence with repository" will print any correspondence you have had with each repository. You can choose to print correspondence you have sent to or received from the repository, and can ask RootsMagic to print the full details for the correspondence.

"Print preparer's name and address" lets you specify whether RootsMagic should print the preparer's name and address at the bottom of the printout. You can set the preparer's name and address in the options screen (page 264).

Source List

The source list will print either a single source, or a list of every source in the database. You can also have RootsMagic print every use (citation) of each source. If you print all sources you can also tell RootsMagic how to sort the printed sources.

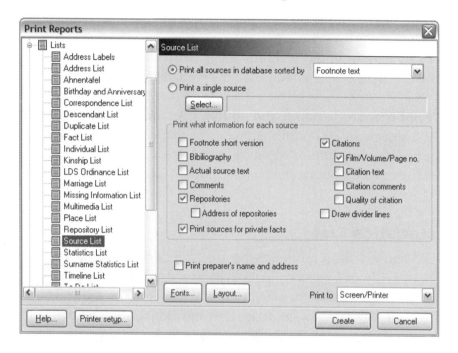

"Footnote short version" will print the short version of the source if it has been entered.

"Bibliography" will print the bibliography version of the source if it has been entered.

You can also choose to print the actual source text and comments about the source.

"Repositories" will print the primary and seconday repository for each source in the list. You can also have RootsMagic print the full address for each repository.

"Print sources for private facts" lets you choose whether RootsMagic should include any facts (birth, death, etc.) that you have marked as "private".

"Citations" specifies whether all citations for each source should be printed. The citation includes the person (or family) and the fact. You can also choose to include the page number, citation text, citation comments, and citation quality for each citation.

"Draw divider lines" will print a line between each repository in the list. This can often improve the readability of the list.

"Print preparer's name and address" lets you specify whether RootsMagic should print the preparer's name and address at the bottom of the printout. You can set the preparer's name and address in the options screen (page 264).

Statistics List

The statistics list is a fun little list that will calculate various statistics about a group of people in your database. It will calculate the minimum, maximum, and averages for age at first marriage, age at death, marriages per individual, and children per marriage. It also breaks these categories down by sex.

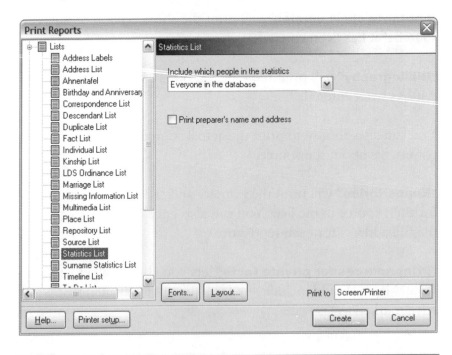

"Include which people in the statistics" lets you decide which people you want to include in the list. If you check "Select individuals", RootsMagic will bring up a list of every person in your database when you click the **"OK"** button. This selection screen is described in the chapter titled "Custom Reports" (page 181), and allows you to select the people you want in your list.

"Print preparer's name and address" lets you specify whether RootsMagic should print the preparer's name and address at the bottom of the printout. You can set the preparer's name and address in the options screen (page 264).

Surname Statistics List

The Surname Statistics List prints a list of every surname in your database. Each surname is listed only once, along with the number of people with that surname (broken down by males and females), and the earliest year and most recent year the surname appears in your database.

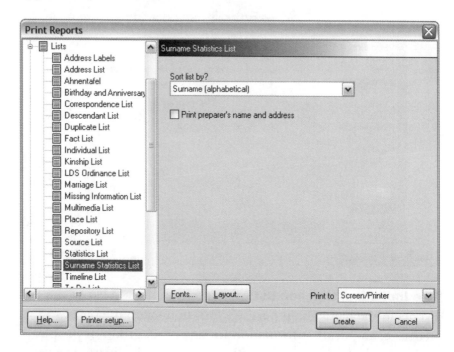

You can sort the surname statistics list: 1) alphabetically, 2) by the number of people with that surname (frequency), 3) by the number of males with that surname, 4) by the number of females with that surname, 5) by the earliest occurrence of the surname, and 6) by the most recent occurrence of the surname.

"Print preparer's name and address" lets you specify whether RootsMagic should print the preparer's name and address at the bottom of the printout. You can set the preparer's name and address in the options screen (page 264).

Timeline List

The Timeline list is actually two different lists that print a chronological list of events for a group of people (including your entire database if desired).

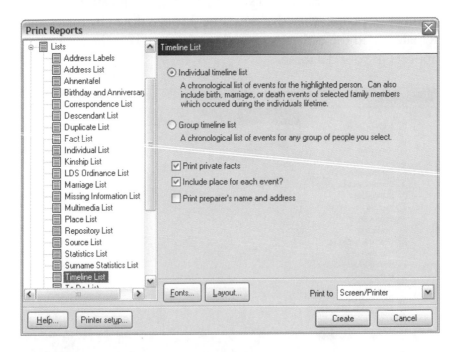

The Individual timeline list prints a chronological list of the events in the highlighted person's life, along with the birth, marriage, and death information for any other group of people that you select (but only those that fall within the lifetime of the primary person). By selecting the family members of the highlighted person, you can get an informative list of all family events which occurred within his or her lifetime.

The Family timeline list simply prints a list of every event for any group of people you select. This is especially useful for printing a list of all events for a family.

RootsMagic will display a list of all the people in your database, and you can select which people you want to include in your Family timeline list. This selection screen is described in the chapter titled "Custom Reports" (page 181).

RootsMagic will then chronologically list all events in the selected person's lives (if they have a date).

"Print private facts" lets you choose whether RootsMagic should include any facts (birth, death, etc.) that you have marked as "private".

"Include place for each event" tells RootsMagic to print the place for each event.

"Print preparer's name and address" lets you specify whether RootsMagic should print the preparer's name and address at the bottom of the printout. You can set the preparer's name and address in the options screen (page 264).

To Do List

The to-do list will print a list of the to-do tasks in your database. It will include the task description, the person the task is for, the soundex code for the person, the repository where the task needs to be done, and the date the task was created.

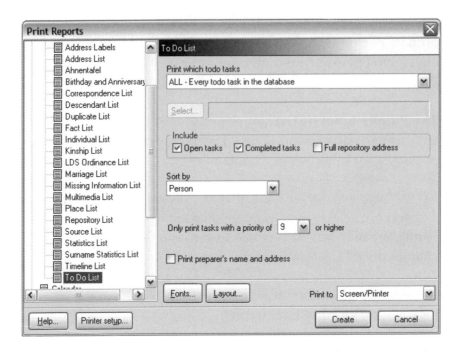

"Print which todo tasks" lets you tell RootsMagic which to-do tasks to print. You have a wide range of choices.

> **All** – This option will print every todo task in your database.
> **General** – This option will print to-do tasks which are not tied to a person or family. These would be tasks you added directly to the To do list ("Lists, To do list").
> **People** – This option will print to-do tasks which are linked to people. RootsMagic will display a list of all the people in your database, and you can select which people you want to include. This selection screen is described in the chapter titled "Custom Reports" (page 181).
> **Person** – This option will print all the todo tasks for a single person. The "Select" button will be enabled for you to choose which person's tasks to print.
> **Family** – This option will print all the todo tasks for a family. The "Select" button will be enabled for you to choose which family's tasks to print.

➢ **Repository** – This option will print all the todo tasks for a repository. The "Select" button will be enabled for you to choose which repository's tasks to print.

➢ **Single** – This option will print a single todo task. The "Select" button will be enabled for you to choose which task to print.

"Sort list by?" lets you sort the to do list by Person (alphabetical by name), task description, repository, or date.

"Open tasks" and **"Completed tasks"** lets you print only the unfinished tasks, only the finished tasks, or both.

"Full repository address" tells RootsMagic to print the full street address for each repository.

"Only print tasks with a priority of X or higher" lets you filter the list to print only the most urgent tasks. You can choose what priority level (and above) you are interested in.

"Print preparer's name and address" lets you specify whether RootsMagic should print the preparer's name and address at the bottom of the printout. You can set the preparer's name and address in the options screen (page 264).

Calendars

If you are always forgetting birthdays and anniversaries, then this is the report for you. You can print a calendar with birthdays and anniversaries for any month or year.

"Calendar(s) to print" lets you select which month (or all months) and which year to print a calendar for. If you choose "All months" then RootsMagic will print a calendar for each month in the year you choose.

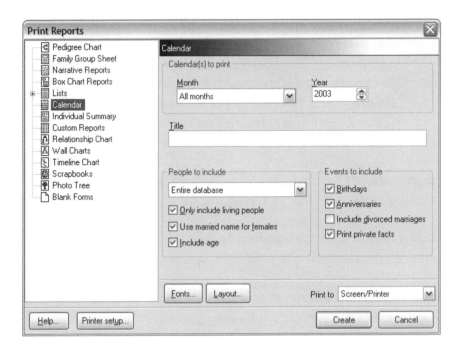

"Title" lets you enter a title for your calendar.

"People to include" lets you print everyone in your database, or just selected people. If you choose to select a group of people, RootsMagic will display a list of all the people in your database, and you can select which people you want to include. This selection screen is described in the chapter titled "Custom Reports" (page 181).

You can also filter to include only living people, print females with their married name, and include the age of each person.

"Events to include" lets you choose whether to print birthdays, anniversaries, or both. You can even choose to ignore anniversaries of marriages with divorces entered.

"Print private facts" lets you choose whether RootsMagic should include any facts (birth, death, etc.) that you have marked as "private".

Individual Summary

The Individual Summary prints just about everything you have entered for a person. You can print a summary for the highlighted person, or you can print multiple summaries all at once. If you choose "Selected individuals", RootsMagic will display a list of all the people in your database, and you can select which people you want to include. The selection screen is described in the chapter titled "Custom Reports" (page 181).

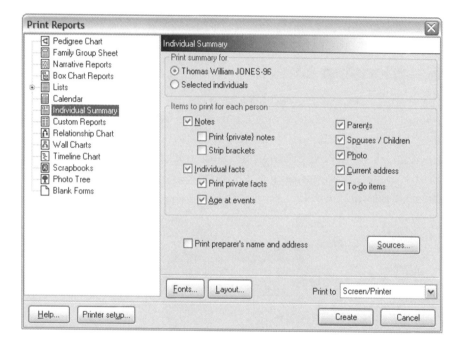

"Items to print for each person" lets you select which items to print for the person. You can include notes, facts (birth, death, etc), the person's age at each event, parents, spouses and children, a photo, to-do list items, and the person's current address. You can also choose whether to print private notes or facts.

The "Sources" button lets you tell RootsMagic how to print sources for the summary (if at all). It will bring up the source print option dialog described on page 110.

"Print preparer's name and address" lets you specify whether RootsMagic should print the preparer's name and address at the bottom of the printout. You can set the preparer's name and address in the options screen (page 264).

Custom Reports

Custom reports allow you to create your own lists. While they are easy to create, there are also sophisticated techniques that can be applied, so we will cover them in detail in the chapter titled "Custom Reports" (page 174).

Relationship Chart

If you have ever wondered how two people in your database are related, then the Relationship Chart is the printout for you. Select the "Relationship Chart" item in the Report dialog. You can select any two people from your database, set some options, and RootsMagic will generate a box chart that shows you exactly how the two people are related.

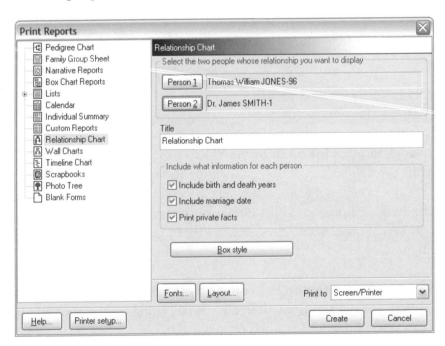

Select the two people whose relationship you want to display - Click on each button to select the two people you want to find the relationship for. RootsMagic will bring up a list of everyone in your database for you to select from. By default, the first person will be set to the person who was highlighted on the main screen, but you can change to a different person if you want.

"Title" lets you enter the title you want printed at the top of the chart.

"Include birth and death years" tells RootsMagic to print the life span for each person (like "1780 – 1843").

"Include marriage date" tells RootsMagic to print the marriage date for each couple in the relationship chart.

"Print private facts" lets you choose whether RootsMagic should include any facts (birth, death, etc.) that you have marked as "private".

"Box style" lets you choose the format of the borders RootsMagic draws around people. This is described in detail on page 119.

Wall Charts

As you add more people to your database, you will find that the connections between people can become blurred in your mind. Wall charts let you print huge family trees which can help you visualize these complicated relationships. While they are easy to create, RootsMagic provides numerous customization tools, so we will cover them in detail in the chapter titled "Wallcharts and Timelines" (page 158).

Timeline Charts

The Timeline chart displays a graphical representation of how the lives of people in your database relate to each other. RootsMagic prints color bars for the lifetime of each person (all or selected) in your database. While they are easy to create, RootsMagic provides numerous customization tools, so we will cover them in detail in the chapter titled "Wallcharts and Timelines" (page 158).

Scrapbook

The Scrapbook is designed to print all the photos for the highlighted person, family, source or place. If you print a scrapbook for a person or family, you can also choose whether you want to include photos attached to the facts for that person or family.

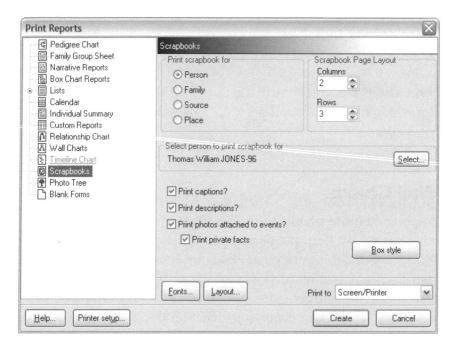

You can select how many rows and columns to print on each page, and whether you want to print the captions or descriptions for each photo. You can tell RootsMagic whether you want a photo included in the scrapbook when you add or edit it in the multimedia scrapbook.

"Print private facts" lets you choose whether RootsMagic should include any facts (birth, death, etc.) that you have marked as "private".

"Select person to print scrapbook for" lets you select the person whose scrapbook you want to print. You can click the "Select" button to change this person. When you choose to print a scrapbook for a family, source, or place, this will let you select the family, source or place to print the scrapbook for.

"Box style" lets you choose the format of the borders RootsMagic draws around photos. This is described in detail on page 119.

Photo Tree

The Photo tree will print a tree (with leaves) with three generations of photos superimposed on it. The tree includes the starting person, his parents, and grandparents. In addition, you can include the brothers and sisters of the start person at the base of the tree.

"Starting person" is the person who the report will begin with. You can click the "Select" button to change this person.

"Title" lets you enter the title you want printed at the top of the photo tree.

"Background image" lets you choose what picture you want as the background of the photo tree. If you leave this field blank, RootsMagic will use a default drawing of a tree.

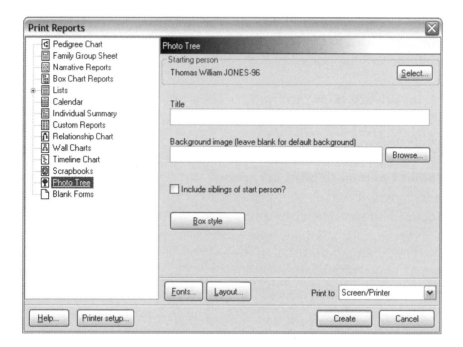

"Include siblings of start person" tells RootsMagic to print all the children at the base of the tree. RootsMagic will reduce the size of the children's photos as necessary to fit them all in the space available.

"Box style" lets you choose the format of the borders RootsMagic draws around the photos. This is described in detail on page 119.

Blank Forms

RootsMagic provides a number of blank forms which you can print. Select the **"Blank Forms"** item in the Report dialog, and choose from the available blank forms.

The **Pedigree Charts** and **Family Group Sheet** look exactly like the normal ones RootsMagic prints, except that they contain no data.

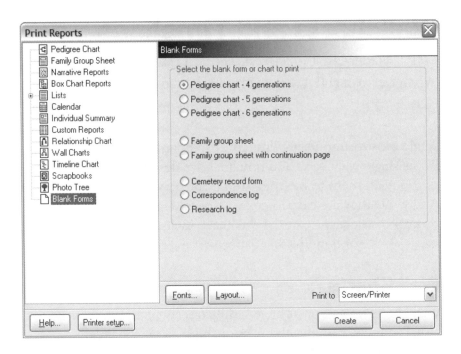

The **Cemetery Records Form**, **Correspondence Log**, and **Research Log** are simply blank forms that you can fill out by hand to keep track of that type of information.

Wallcharts and Timelines

Call it a clan, call it a network, call it a tribe, call it a family.
Whatever you call it, whoever you are, you need one.

- Jane Howard, "Families"

While most printouts are limited to standard sized pages, RootsMagic wallcharts and timelines are designed to be as large as you need them to be (they aren't called *wall*charts for nothing). And while they are easy to create, RootsMagic gives you full control over every aspect of the chart, including the positioning, size, colors, fonts, and other aspects of every object in the chart.

Wall Charts

Wall charts let you print huge family trees which can help you visualize these complicated relationships. You can create ancestor, descendant, or hourglass wallcharts. To create a wallchart, click the "Reports" button on the toolbar, or choose "Reports, Charts, Wallcharts" from the menu.

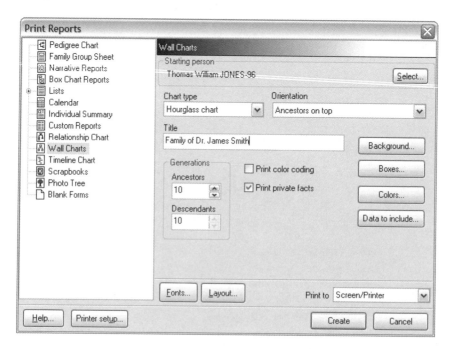

"Starting person" is the person who the chart will begin with. You can click the "Select" button to change this person.

"Chart type" lets you select what type of chart you want to print.
- ➤ **Ancestor chart** - Prints a chart of the starting person and his/her ancestors (parents, grandparents, etc). Only direct ancestors are included in the chart.
- ➤ **Descendant chart** - Prints a chart of the starting person and his/her descendants (children, grandchildren, etc).
- ➤ **Hourglass chart** - Prints a chart which includes both the ancestors and descendants of the starting person.

"Orientation" lets you choose which direction the chart is laid out. For example, ancestor charts can go from left to right (the default), or from right to left, top to bottom, or bottom to top. The options will vary depending on which Chart type you select.

"Title" lets you enter the title for the top of your chart.

"Generations" lets you specify how many generations you want to include in your chart. If you choose an ancestor or descendant chart the appropriate generations field will be enabled. If you choose an hourglass chart you will be able to select the number of ancestor and descendant generations separately.

"Print color coding" lets you print any color coding you may have applied to people in your database. If you mark this checkbox, RootsMagic will color a person's box in the same color as they are color coded on screen. The boxes of non color coded people will be printed in the default color chosen in the "Colors" dialog. Color coding is described on page 226.

"Print private facts" lets you choose whether RootsMagic should include any facts (birth, death, etc.) that you have marked as "private".

The "Background" button lets you choose the background for your chart.

You can choose no background, a solid color, or even select an image as the background. Just remember that while a colored or image background can really look nice, it can also use a huge amount of ink when printing. Companies that print wallcharts on large plotters almost always charge much more for charts with color or image backgrounds.

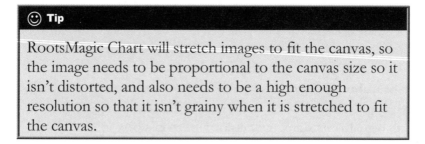

☺ **Tip**

RootsMagic Chart will stretch images to fit the canvas, so the image needs to be proportional to the canvas size so it isn't distorted, and also needs to be a high enough resolution so that it isn't grainy when it is stretched to fit the canvas.

The "Boxes" button lets you select the size of the boxes for each person, the spacing between the boxes (both horizontally and vertically), as well as whether you want the box to have a drop shadow. When RootsMagic generates the wall chart it will make all of the boxes the size you specify. After the chart is generated you can adjust the size of individual boxes if you want.

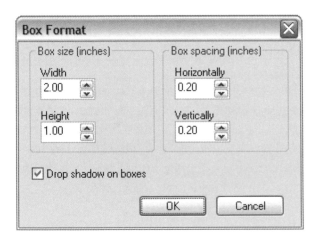

The "Colors" button lets you choose the colors for the various parts of the wall chart. Simply click on one of the buttons and you can select the desired color for each aspect of the chart.

The "Data to include" button is where you can choose exactly what information to put in each person's box. RootsMagic will always print the person's name in the box, and you can choose how that name is formatted.

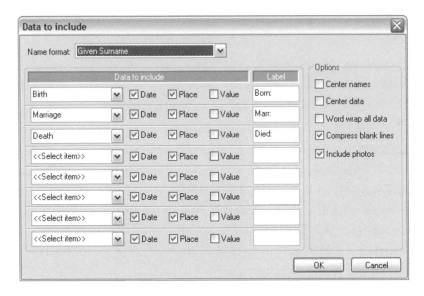

You can also choose which other information to include. You can select up to 8 facts to print for each person, and can specify whether to include the date, place, or value for each fact you choose. You can also change the default label RootsMagic uses for each fact type.

If you choose a lot of information to include, you probably will want to increase the size of the boxes as described earlier, or reduce the size of the fonts using the "Fonts" button on the wall chart dialog. The "Include photos" checkbox lets you include the primary picture for each person. If you include pictures, you might want to consider widening the boxes.

By default, RootsMagic will display each fact on its own line in the person's box, but you can mark the "Word wrap all data" checkbox to cause the data to wrap in the box. If you don't word wrap data, you can choose whether events with no information will print as blank lines or not.

Finally, you can choose to center the person's name and data in the box. If you don't mark these checkboxes, RootsMagic will left justify the name and data.

Timeline Charts

The Timeline chart displays a graphical representation of how the lives of people in your database relate to each other. RootsMagic prints color bars for the lifetime of each person (all or selected) in your database.

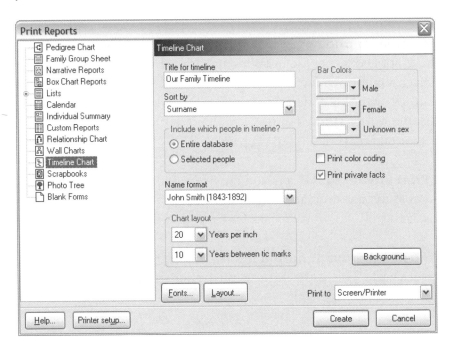

"Title for timeline" lets you enter the title you want to print at the top of your timeline chart.

"Sort by" lets you choose the order (from top to bottom) of the bars for each person. You can choose to sort by the person's surname or birthdate.

"Include which people in timeline" lets you choose whether to include everyone or to choose a group of people. If you choose to include only selected people RootsMagic will bring up the selection screen described on page 181.

"Name format" lets you choose how you want each person's name printed on the chart.

"Chart layout" lets you choose the spacing which RootsMagic will use between tic marks.

"Bar colors" lets you select the color of the bars for males, females, and people with no sex entered.

"Print color coding" lets you print any color coding you may have applied to people in your database. If you mark this checkbox, RootsMagic will color a person's bar in the same color as they are color coded on screen. The bars of non color coded people will be printed in the default color chosen in "Bar colors". Color coding is described on page 226.

"Print private facts" lets you choose whether RootsMagic should include any facts (birth, death, etc.) that you have marked as "private".

The "Background" button lets you choose the background for your chart. This is the same as the wallchart background button described on page 160.

RootsMagic Chart

After RootsMagic creates a wallchart or timeline, another included program called RootsMagic Chart will open the chart so that you can customize it, print it, or save it to disk to work on later.

RootsMagic Chart gives you full control over the positioning, size, colors, fonts, and other aspects of every object in the chart. With simple mouse control you can resize an individual's box, or drag it to another location on the canvas without breaking the family links. You can change colors of individual boxes, or change the font or color of the text in the boxes.

You can even customize your chart by adding additional text, pictures, or shapes to the chart, and you can change the background image or color.

The Canvas

The canvas is the actual drawing area for your chart. All objects, including person boxes, links between boxes, text, images, and shapes are displayed on the canvas.

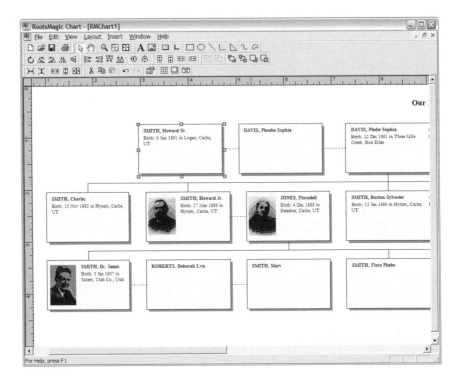

When RootsMagic creates a chart it will use the background image or color you chose when generating the chart, and will automatically size the canvas to fit the chart. If you want to change the size or background in RootsMagic Chart, you can do that as well.

To change the size of the canvas, do "Layout > Canvas size" from the menu, then enter the height and width of the canvas in inches. This is useful when you rearrange the items in the chart and need more (or less) room to handle the changes.

To change the background of the canvas, do "Layout > Background" from the menu, and RootsMagic Chart will display the same dialog as when you originally created the chart (page 160). RootsMagic Chart also provides a number of modes for viewing your data on the canvas. Simply click one of the buttons on the zoom toolbar to choose what mode you are in.

Select – Changes the cursor to the default "Select" cursor which lets you select, move, and size objects.

Pan – Changes the cursor to the "Pan" cursor (which looks like a hand). When this cursor is selected you can click and drag the entire canvas rather than individual objects. To exit from Pan mode just click on the Select button on the toolbar.

Zoom – Changes the cursor to the "Zoom" cursor (which looks like a magnifying glass). When this cursor is selected, clicking the mouse button will zoom in on the canvas, while right clicking the mouse button will zoom out from the canvas.

Zoom to fit – Causes RootsMagic Chart to zoom so that the entire chart is visible on the screen. For large charts this can be used as an overview, but can be very difficult to use for actual work.

Zoom to selection – Causes RootsMagic Chart to zoom so that all selected objects fill the screen.

Toggle grid – Turns the "grid" on or off. The grid is simply a grid of dots which displays on the canvas, but does not actually print. It is useful to help line things up when you are moving objects.

Snap to grid – When snap to grid is enabled, objects will snap to the nearest grid dot (both horizontally and vertically) when moving and resizing the object. This limits the precision of how boxes are sized and positioned, but is very useful for keeping items exactly lined up.

Toggle page bounds – When this is enabled, lines will be drawn to show how the chart would be broken if printed to a regular (small page) printer. This can be useful if you want to print a chart that will be printed on smaller pages and taped together to help you avoid printing boxes or other objects over a page break.

Manipulating Objects

The ability to manipulate any individual item or object on the canvas gives you the flexibility to completely customize any RootsMagic chart. These objects can be person boxes, pictures or text that you may have added, or other shapes like rectangles and circles.

Adding Objects

To add a new object on the canvas, choose Insert from the menu, or click one of the buttons on the drawing toolbar.

> **Text** – Lets you add a text object to the canvas. The cursor will turn into the "add text" cursor, and clicking on the canvas will drop the new text object onto the canvas.
> **Picture** – Lets you add an image to the canvas. A file dialog will open to let you select the image you want to add. Select the desired image and click "Open" and RootsMagic Chart will change the cursor to the "Add picture" cursor, and clicking on the canvas will drop the picture onto the canvas.

➢ **Person box** – Lets you add a new person box to the canvas. The cursor will turn into the "add object" cursor, and clicking on the canvas will drop the new person box onto the canvas. You can then double click the name text or event text to change it.

➢ **Link** – Lets you link two person boxes together. The cursor will turn into the "add link" cursor (which looks like a little plus sign). When you move the cursor over a spot that the link can be attached (on the middle of any side of a person box) the cursor will change to a circle with a plus sign in it. You can then click the mouse and the link will attach to the person box in that location. You can then move the cursor to the side of another person box (where the circle cursor again appears) and click to finish the link.

➢ **Rectangle** – Lets you add a rectangle to the canvas. You can then click on the canvas, and while holding the mouse down drag out the size of the rectangle you want. When you release the mouse the rectangle will be added to the canvas. If you want a perfect square, hold the shift key down while sizing the rectangle.

➢ **Ellipse** – Lets you add an ellipse to the canvas. You can then click on the canvas, and while holding the mouse down drag out the size of the ellipse you want. When you release the mouse the ellipse will be added to the canvas. If you want a perfect circle, hold the shift key down while sizing the ellipse.

➢ **Line** – Lets you add a line to the canvas. You can then click on the canvas, and while holding the mouse down drag out the line you want. When you release the mouse the line will be added to the canvas.

➢ **Line (multi-segment)** – Lets you add a multi-segment line to the canvas. You can then click on the canvas where you want the line to start. Then move the mouse and click on the endpoint of each segment. When you are ready to finish, double click the mouse to set the last segment of the line.

- ➢ **Polygon** – Lets you add a polygon to the canvas. You can then click on the canvas where you want the polygon to start. Then move the mouse and click on the endpoint of each segment. When you are ready to finish, double click the mouse to set the last segment of the line.
- ➢ **Curve** – This works almost exactly the same as adding a multi-segment line, except that RootsMagic Chart will "fit" a curve to the line segments.
- ➢ **Closed curve** – This works almost exactly the same as adding a polygon, except that RootsMagic Chart will "fit" a curve to the line segments.

Selecting Objects

To select an object, simply click on the object with your mouse. RootsMagic Chart will display sizing handles (tiny squares on each side and corner of the object) to show that the object is selected.

To select multiple objects you can click on the first object, then hold down the Shift key on the keyboard while you click the remaining objects. If the objects are close together you can click and drag a region around the objects and all objects inside that rectangular region will be selected.

Moving Objects

To move any object on the canvas, simply click the object with the mouse and drag it to the new position, then release the mouse button. If more than one item is currently selected, this will move all selected items at once.

Resizing Objects

To resize any object on the canvas, click once on the item to display the sizing handles. You can then click on any of these handles and drag them to resize the object (either larger or smaller).

Changing Object Properties

To change the properties of an object (such as color, font, or line style) right click the mouse on the object and select "Properties" from the pop up menu. For most objects the property dialog will appear where you can change any of the properties of the item. If you select Properties for a person box, a list of the components of the person box will appear (box, shadow, name text, event text) and you can change the properties of each of those parts individually.

Positioning Objects

RootsMagic Chart offers many commands to help you size and position objects on the canvas beyond the click and drag method. You can access these commands from the "Layout" menu or by clicking the appropriate button on the toolbar.

Align – The align functions will align all selected objects with the "primary" selected object (the one with the gray sizing handles). You can align the left or right sides, the tops, the bottoms, or the centers (either vertically or horizontally).

Space evenly / Make same size – These commands will evenly space multiple objects, or will make all the selected objects the same size.

- **Across** – Will horizontally space all of the selected objects between the left-most and the right-most selected object.

- **Down** – Will vertically space all of the selected objects between the upper-most and lowest selected object.

- **Width** – Will make all selected objects the same width as the "primary" selected object (the one with the gray sizing handles).

- **Height** – Will make all selected objects the same height as the "primary" selected object (the one with the gray sizing handles).

- **Both** – Will make all selected objects the same size (both height and width) as the "primary" selected object (the one with the gray sizing handles).

Nudge – The nudge commands will move the selected object (or objects) just a tiny bit. This is useful when an object is very close to the position you want but just needs a little bit of a "nudge". You can nudge objects up, down, left or right.

Grouping / Order – Moves the selected object in front of or in back of other objects on the canvas.

- **Group** – Combines all selected objects into a single new object (group). When this new grouped object is moved, sized or otherwise manipulated, all parts of the group are manipulated equally.

- **Ungroup** – Breaks apart a group of objects which were combined using the Group command.

- **To Front** – Moves the selected object in front of all other objects on the canvas.

- **To Back** – Moves the selected object behind all other objects on the canvas.

- **Forward one** – Moves the selected object one step towards the front of the canvas.

- **Backward one**– Moves the selected object one step towards the back of the canvas.

⟳ ⛛ ⛛ ⛛ ⛛ **Rotate / Flip** – The rotate and flip commands let you rotate the selected object.

- **Rotate** – Lets you rotate the selected object. After selecting this option the mouse pointer will change to the rotate pointer. Clicking and dragging on the corner of an object will rotate the object as desired.

- **Rotate left** – Rotates the selected object 90 degrees to the left.

- **Rotate right** – Rotates the selected object 90 degrees to the right.

- **Flip vertical** – Flips the selected object vertically.

- **Flip horizontal** – Flips the selected object horizontally.

Working with Files

One of the biggest advantages of a separate charting program like RootsMagic Chart is that you can save your modified chart to disk, and later reopen it to print it or edit it some more. RootsMagic Chart offers all the standard file commands, like:

- **New** – Opens a new blank chart / canvas on the screen.
- **Open** – Brings up a file dialog where you can select an existing RootsMagic chart to be opened on screen.
- **Close** – Closes the currently active window.
- **Save** – Lets you save the current chart to disk. If you have not yet saved the chart, a file dialog will come up where you can enter the file name for the chart. If the chart has already been saved once, this button will just save the modified chart with the existing name.
- **Save as** – Lets you save a copy of the current chart with another name. This is useful if you want to make a copy of a chart for special modification.

- **Export** – Lets you export the chart to a number of graphics formats. You can export to an Enhanced Meta File (*.emf) file, which is a resizable format that can be used to print on large plotters. There are also a number of standard image formats (.jpg, .png, etc) so you can create images of your chart.

If you want to run RootsMagic Chart to open a previously created chart, simply start the program with the icon installed on your desktop or in the Windows Start menu.

Printing Your Chart

Of course the final destination for your wall chart is the printer. RootsMagic Chart offers several options for printing your chart.

If you print your chart to a regular printer, the chart will be broken up and printed on pages which you can then tape together into a larger chart. If you want to see how the pages will be broken up before you print the chart, choose "View, Page bounds" from the menu to toggle lines on the screen which show where the pages would fall. You can also do "File, Print preview" to see exactly what each page will look like when printing.

If you are lucky enough to own a printer capable of printing a chart the size you need, you can do "File, Page setup" to choose the printer and the larger paper size to print on. RootsMagic Chart will automatically print to the larger page size.

Finally, you can also go to www.PrintMyChart.com, or do "Reports, PrintMyChart.com" from the RootsMagic menu (not the RootsMagic Chart menu) and take advantage of the chart printing service offered by RootsMagic, Inc. The price to print your chart will depend on the size of the chart, and whether the chart has pictures and / or a background color or image. You can see the size of the chart by doing "File, Properties" from the RootsMagic Chart menu.

Custom Reports

Have it your way...

If you want to get a list of information from RootsMagic in a particular format, but it isn't available in the program, then the custom report creator is the place to go. The Custom Report creator is probably one of the most powerful features of RootsMagic. You can create your own customized lists that include almost any information about anyone in your database, sorted in any order and laid out in any position

Let's Create One

The easiest way to learn about custom reports is just to create one. Let's say you want a list of people in your database along with their birth and death place. When it is finished, you want it to look something like this:

Name	Birth Date	Birth Place
Doe, John	3 Sep 1906	Albuquerque, New Mexico
Doe, Mary	10 May 1943	Provo, Utah
Jones, David	8 Aug 1920	Phoenix, Arizona
Smith, William	4 Feb 1872	Columbia, Missouri
Thomas, Bill	12 Jul 1889	Pittsburgh, Pennsylvania

To design such a report, you will need to tell RootsMagic that for each person, you want to print from left to right the name, then the birth date, and finally the birth place. You will also need to tell RootsMagic to print the words "Name", "Birth Date", and "Birth Place" in the header at the top of each column. Let's create this report now.

To create a custom report, click the Printer button on the toolbar, then select "Custom Reports" from the list on the Report dialog. The two main aspects of creating a custom report are designing the report, and selecting the people to print in the report.

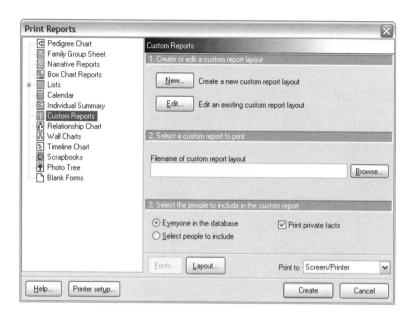

Designing a Custom Report

To start creating our custom report, click the **"New"** button on the dialog. RootsMagic will display the screen where we will design our report. On this screen, we will tell RootsMagic what information we want to print for each person, and where to print it on the page.

The Custom Report Designer is divided into two sections, the header and the details.

The Header

The Header is where you will enter text that you want to print at the top of each page.

To add text to the header, click your mouse on the **"Add Text"** button and type the word **Name** into the dialog that appears. Then click the OK button.

RootsMagic will put the text you entered in the upper left corner of the header section. You can click on the text with your mouse and drag it to the position in the header where you want it to print. If the text is too long, you can also click on the text to make "handles" appear. Handles are little dots that surround the text. You can click on the handles and drag them to resize the text so that it all shows.

Now just repeat this action to add **"Birth Date"** and **"Birth Place"**, and drag them to the desired position in the header (as shown in the Custom Report Designer screen shot on the previous page).

To edit a text field once it is on the screen, double click on the text. RootsMagic will allow you to edit the text.

To delete some text, click on the text, then press the **"Del"** key on your keyboard. RootsMagic will ask if you really want to delete the item. Click **"Yes"**.

The Details

The Details section is where you enter the information that you want to print for each person. Anything you put in the details section will be printed once for every person that you include in the custom report.

In our case, we want to print the name, birth date, and birth place for every person, so we need to tell RootsMagic to print those three items for each person. We do this by adding "fields". Think of a "field" as a place-holder that RootsMagic will fill in with real data for each person.

To add a field to the detail section, click your mouse on the "Add Field" button. A list of available fields will appear.

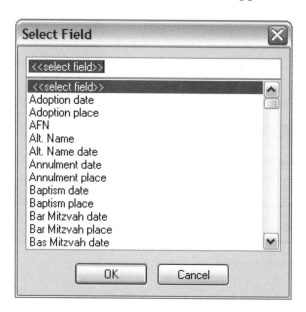

Since the person's name is the first item we want to print, select Name – 'Surname, Given' from the list, then click OK. The new field will be displayed in the upper left corner of the details section. It will be displayed in a different color than the text you added in the header, but you can move and resize it exactly the same way you do the text.

Now just repeat this action to add fields for Birth date and Birth place, and drag them to the desired position in the details section (as shown in the Custom Report Designer screen shot earlier). As you add new fields, they may drop on top of existing fields. Don't worry about that, just click on the new field and drag it to the desired position.

To delete a field, click on the field, then press the "Del" key on your keyboard. RootsMagic will ask if you really want to delete the item. Click "Yes".

Custom Report Options

RootsMagic offers a number of options that apply to your custom report. Click the "Options" button to bring up the following screen. When you have selected the options you want, click the OK button to return to the Custom Report Designer screen.

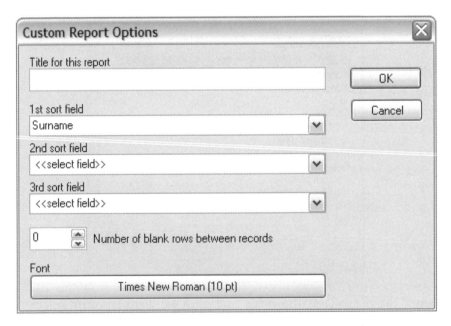

"Title for this report" is where you type the title you want to appear at the top of your custom report. For example, you might enter "Birth List" for the report we are creating now.

"1st sort field" is where you tell RootsMagic how you want your report sorted. Select the sort order from the drop list. We can just pick "Surname" for this list, since we want the list to be sorted alphabetically by last name. If we later wanted to sort the list by birth date or birth place, we can change the sort order here.

"2nd sort field" and **"3rd sort field"** let you further sort the list. For example, if you set the 2nd sort field to "Birth date", then all the "John Smiths" who were grouped together by the "Surname" sort, will be sorted amongst themselves by birth date.

"Number of blank rows between records" lets you tell RootsMagic how to space individuals in your custom report. If you use the default value of 0, RootsMagic will print each person's information on one line after another. If you change this value to 1, RootsMagic will put 1 blank line between each person that it prints.

"Font" lets you select the font that RootsMagic will use to print your custom report. Click on the button and select the font and font size from the standard Windows font selection dialog. The font you select will be displayed on the button.

To save your custom report once it is designed, click the "Close" button at the top of the Custom Report Designer. RootsMagic will ask if you want to save your report. You must save your report if you want to print it, so click "Yes". The standard Windows file dialog will appear so that you can save the report to a file. RootsMagic will then display the filename of the report you designed in the custom report dialog as the report to print.

Once you have designed a custom report, you can reuse the same report over and over without having to redesign it.

Modifying a Custom Report

If you ever need to make changes to a custom report, click the "Edit" button and select the report file using the standard Windows file dialog. If you have previously printed a custom report, RootsMagic will use that filename as the default in the file open dialog.

RootsMagic will load the selected report and open it in the Custom Report Designer. You can then add, move, resize or delete text or fields. You can also change the options like title, font and sort order. When you are satisfied with the changes, click the "Close" button and RootsMagic will ask you to save the changed report.

Printing a Custom Report

When you are ready to print a custom report that you have designed, enter the name of the report file in the custom report dialog by typing it in or by clicking the "Browse" button and selecting the report file using the standard Windows file dialog.

You can print the custom report to either your screen (which will let you print it) or to a text file. If you select a text file, RootsMagic will ask you for a file name, and will save the custom report as a "tab delimited" file (meaning that tabs separate every field). You can also print to a comma delimited file as well. While these formats aren't particularly readable, they are perfect for importing into spreadsheets or database programs.

Also, before clicking the "Create" button to begin creating the custom report, you need to decide if you want to print the report for everyone in your database, or if you only want to select only certain individuals. You can also choose whether to include any facts you have marked as private.

Printing a Report of Every Person

If you select **"Everyone in the database"** before clicking the **"Create"** button, RootsMagic will generate the custom report and display it on the screen in a print preview. From this print preview, you can zoom, change pages, or print the report.

Selecting People to Print in Your Report

If you choose **"Select people to include"** and then click the **"Create"** button, RootsMagic will ask you to select the individuals you want before it generates the report. The following "selection screen" will appear.

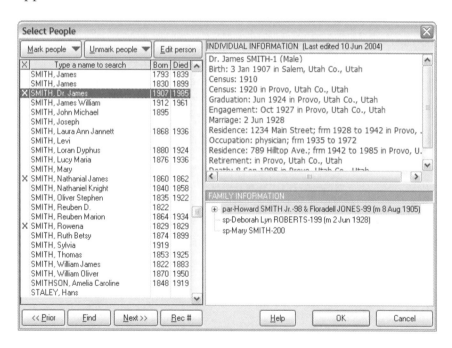

As with the RootsMagic Explorer (page 60) you can type a person's name to highlight them and you can edit the highlighted person. But the main purpose of the selection screen is to select a group of people.

This selection screen allows you to "mark" and "unmark" people to include in your custom report. When a person is marked, an "x" appears in front of their name in the list. When you unmark a person, the "x" is removed from in front of their name. You simply mark and unmark people until you have an "x" next to every person you want to include. Then click the OK button and RootsMagic will generate the custom report for you.

There are two buttons at the top of the selection screen, "Mark people" and "Unmark people". Clicking each button will display a menu of ways you can mark (or unmark) people in the list.

To mark or unmark a single person, highlight the person in the list, and choose "Person" from either the "Mark" or "Unmark" menu. You can also just double click on the person's name in the list to toggle the "x" on and off.

To mark or unmark a family, highlight a person and select "Family" from either the "Mark" or "Unmark" menu. If the person is only in one family (whether as a parent or child), RootsMagic will mark (or unmark) each person in the family. If the person is a member of more than one family, RootsMagic will present a list like this and allow you to select which family you want to mark or unmark.

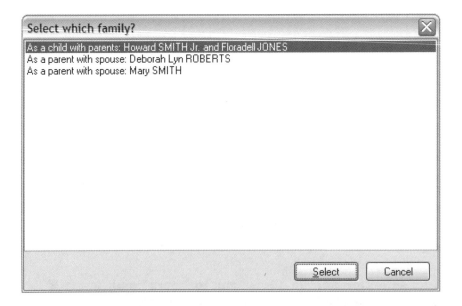

To mark or unmark a person and their ancestors, highlight the person and select **"Ancestors of highlighted person"** from either the "Mark" or "Unmark" menu.

You can choose the number of generations to consider, and whether to include the children of each ancestor as well. You can also choose to print the collateral lines which tries to select all ancestors and their families.

Make your choices, then click OK and RootsMagic will mark or unmark the highlighted person and his or her ancestors.

To mark or unmark a person and their descendants, highlight the person and select **"Descendants of highlighted person"** from the "Mark" or "Unmark" menu.

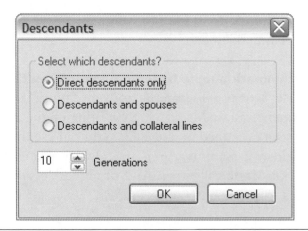

You can choose the number of generations to consider, and whether to include the spouses of each descendant as well. You can also choose to print the collateral lines which tries to select all descendants and their families.

Make your choices, then click OK and RootsMagic will mark or unmark the highlighted person and his or her descendants.

To mark or unmark everyone in the database, select "Everyone in the database" from either the "Mark" or "Unmark" menu.

> ☺ **Tip**
>
> The "Everyone" option is especially useful when you want to include everybody except for a certain few. You can mark everyone in your database, then use the other options to unmark those few that you don't want included.

To mark or unmark everyone related to the highlighted person, select "Everyone in person's tree" from either the "Mark" or "Unmark" menu. RootsMagic will mark or unmark everyone in the same tree as the highlighted person.

To mark or unmark living people, select "Living people" from the "Mark" or "Unmark" menu.

To mark or unmark dead people, select "Dead people" from the "Mark" or "Unmark" menu.

To mark or unmark people based on any information about them, choose "Select people by data fields" from the "Mark" or "Unmark" menu. RootsMagic will then bring up the exact same "Search" screen described on page 62. You can use this screen to enter any fields you want to search in, and what you want to find in them. RootsMagic will either mark or unmark every person that matches what you enter in this screen.

Publishing Your Family History

This is where is all comes together.

If you have ever tried to print several different books or charts, and then tried to combine them into a single book, you know what a pain it is trying to get everything working together.

The RootsMagic Publisher allows you to combine multiple reports into a single document (or book). This document can include narrative books (like the modified register), pedigree charts, family group sheets, and several other common printouts. The document can also include cover and title pages, a table of contents, other introductory pages, a shared index and source bibliography covering all the sections in the document.

To create a book, click the "Publish" button on the toolbar, or select **"Reports, Publisher"** from the main menu, and the following dialog will appear.

You will first need to create a book template by clicking the "New" button. You can enter the filename and RootsMagic will display it across the top of the Publisher dialog. If you want to open an existing book template click the "Open" button and select it from the file dialog. You must have a book template file selected (either new or open) before you can begin adding chapters or making other selections.

To add a new chapter to your book, click the "Add a chapter" button. A menu will appear which lets you select the type of chapter (pedigree chart, narrative report, etc). RootsMagic will then bring up the selection screen for you to choose the starting person for the chapter, and will then bring up the settings dialog for that chapter type. This dialog will be basically the same as when you print a single copy of that chart or report.

In addition, you can add a text chapter which will bring up the following dialog where you can enter your own title and free form text.

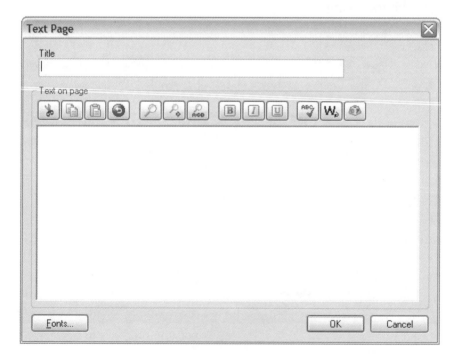

You can also add blank pages, which is useful if you want to add photos or other items to your book which aren't stored in RootsMagic.

The chapter will initially be added at the end of the chapter list, but you can use the **"Up"** and **"Down"** buttons to put it in the desired position.

⚫ Warning

When you create a book template, the chapters you add are specific to people in the current database. For example, you can add a pedigree chart for John Doe, or a narrative book for Mary Smith.

Creating a book template created for one database with a different database can lead to unexpected results, since the people in the other database are not the same ones you created the journal for.

To modify a chapter, highlight the chapter in the list and click the **"Edit"** button. The same dialog that appeared when you added the chapter will allow you to make any changes.

To remove a chapter highlight the chapter and click the **"Delete"** button. RootsMagic will ask you to verify that you want to delete the chapter.

To rearrange the order of chapters in your book click the **"Up"** or **"Down"** buttons to move the highlighted chapter up or down one spot in the list.

The RootsMagic Publisher allow lets you add introductory pages to your book as well. You can enable or disable any of these special pages by clicking the appropriate checkbox. When you enable a special section, RootsMagic will enable the Options button for that section type where you can enter the details for that section.

> **Cover page** – Lets you create a cover page for your book. You can enter a title, subtitle, and can select a photo for the cover page. You can also choose the font for the title and subtitle.
> **Title page** – Lets you create a title page for your book. You can enter a title and subtitle, which are the same as those in the cover page. You can also enter the author and publisher information for your book.
> **Copyright page** – Lets you create a copyright page for your book. RootsMagic will bring up the text page dialog as described earlier, except that the text will be pre-filled with copyright text that you can modify.
> **Dedication, Acknowledgements, and Preface** – Lets you create dedication, acknowledgements, and prefaces pages for your book. RootsMagic will bring up the text page dialog where you can enter a title and the text for the pages, so you aren't strictly limited to these sections. For example, if you don't need a dedication but would like a Foreword instead, you can change the title and text to do that. The title can be centered or left justified.
> **Table of contents** – Lets you create a table of contents for your book. You can choose what fonts to print the table of contents with.

Index options – Lets you choose whether to print an index for the book. This is the same option as described on page 106.

Page layout – Click this button to bring up the Page layout dialog to set the page margins, headers, and other page settings for the document. This is the same dialog as described on page 98.

Source options - Lets you tell RootsMagic how to print sources for the book (if at all). It will bring up the source print option dialog described on page 110.

Print to – Select the destination for the printout. You can print to screen/printer, rich text file (RTF), or Acrobat file (PDF). Some chapter types will not print to RTF, and RootsMagic will notify you about this if you select this option.

To print the book click the "Generate book" button to generate the book using the settings you have chosen.

If you make changes to your database (new people or facts), you can return to the RootsMagic Publisher, and generate the book and it will create the book taking into account any changes you made.

Sharing Data with Others

Share and share alike.

Genealogy is one of the few hobbies where you want to give everything you collect to others (and want them to give theirs to you). RootsMagic lets you share your data with others by providing full GEDCOM import and export, PAF import, Family Origins import, and the ability to create shareable CDs of your database.

Creating a Shareable CD

RootsMagic makes it easy to create a CD of your database to share with others. The CD you create and share will automatically display an introduction page with a title, photo, introduction, and contact information. The introduction page will also have a button which will present your database in a read-only version of RootsMagic. To create a shareable CD, select "Tools, Create a shareable CD" from the menu.

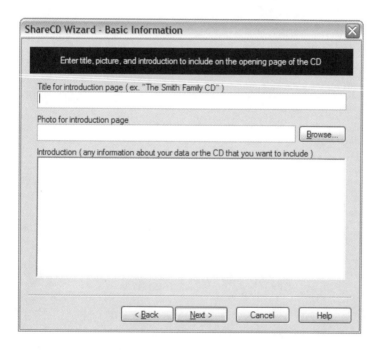

Enter the title, photograph, and introduction for your intro page. If you don't want to choose a photograph, RootsMagic will use a default image. Click the "Next" button to continue.

Enter your contact information; name, address, phone number, email address, and website. You can click the "Preview your CD opening page" button to see what your introduction page will look like. If you see something you need to change, close the preview intro page, make the changes and preview it again.

When you are ready to create your Shareable CD, click the "Finish" button. RootsMagic will organize the files to burn to the CD and will display the "Burn CD" dialog. Make sure you have a blank CD in the drive, select which drive to burn to (if you have more than one), and click the "Burn CD/DVD" button. RootsMagic will create the Shareable CD.

Importing PAF and Family Origins Files

RootsMagic can directly import data from Personal Ancestral File (PAF) version 2 and later, Family Origins version 4 and later, and Family Origins backups version 5 and later. All information will be brought in to RootsMagic, including names, dates, places, links, and notes.

To import data from PAF or Family Origins, create a new database and do **"File, Import, PAF file"** or **"File, Import, Family Origins file"**, or **"File, Import, Family Origins backup"** from the main menu. RootsMagic will bring up the standard Windows file open dialog where you can select the file you want to import.

> ☺ **Tip**
>
> The PAF and Family Origins imports will only read a file into a new (empty) database. This isn't a problem unless you want to combine the data into an existing database. In this case, create a new database and import the file into that database. Then drag and drop the information into your existing database.

What is GEDCOM?

GEDCOM is a file format. It is not a piece of software, although many software programs can read and write GEDCOM files. A GEDCOM filename ends with a .GED extension (like "family.ged").

GEDCOM was developed by the Family History Department of The Church of Jesus Christ of Latter-day Saints (LDS Church) to provide a flexible, uniform format for exchanging computerized genealogical data. GEDCOM is an acronym for **GE**nealogical **D**ata **COM**munication. Its purpose is to foster the sharing of genealogical information and the development of a wide range of inter-operable software products to assist genealogists, historians, and other researchers.

Importing a GEDCOM File

To read data from a GEDCOM file into RootsMagic, you need to import the file. RootsMagic will import all of the information from the file, including names, facts, notes, sources, links, etc.

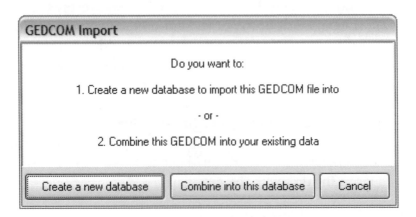 **To import a GEDCOM file**, do "File, Import GEDCOM" from the main menu or click the "Import" button on the toolbar. RootsMagic will display the Windows file dialog so you can select the GEDCOM file you want to import.

If you are importing the file into an existing database, RootsMagic will ask if you want to create a new database to import the GEDCOM into, combine the GEDCOM with the current database, or cancel.

GEDCOM Import

Do you want to:

1. Create a new database to import this GEDCOM file into

- or -

2. Combine this GEDCOM into your existing data

| Create a new database | Combine into this database | Cancel |

If you choose to combine the GEDCOM, RootsMagic will mix all the names in the GEDCOM file with the names already in your database. If the GEDCOM contains names which are already in your database, you will end up with 2 copies of each of those people.

RootsMagic will then display the following dialog, which lets you add a source to each person or event in the GEDCOM file so you can tell where the record came from (only one source is added, and every person or event in the GEDCOM file will point to it).

You can choose to add the source to every person, every fact, every person and fact, or to not add a source. If you choose to add a source, you need to enter the name and address of the person you received the GEDCOM for (in order to create the source).

If a GEDCOM file is too large to fit on a single disk, it may be broken into several smaller files. If you ever import one of these multi-disk GEDCOM files, RootsMagic will automatically ask you to insert the disk with the next part.

When you import a GEDCOM file, it is not linked in any way to the names you already had in your database. It is up to you to connect the new names from the GEDCOM with your existing family tree. If you have duplicate copies of individuals in your database, merging those records will automatically link the trees together. Otherwise, you can use the **"Add, Parents"**, **"Add, Spouse"** and **"Add, Child"** commands to link the individuals together. When RootsMagic asks if you want to create a new person or link to an existing person, select the link option to link the individuals together.

> ☺ **Tip**
>
> While RootsMagic provides a "merge" feature (page 201) it is really hard to remove or merge a lot of unwanted names from your database if you combine in a GEDCOM file you didn't really want.
>
> Instead, you may want to import the GEDCOM file into a new (blank) database, so that you can view the new information to see if you really want it in your database.
>
> **If you do**, you can then import the GEDCOM file into your main database. **If you don't**, you can delete the new database and go back to work with your main database.
>
> **If you only want part of the GEDCOM file in your database**, just drag and drop the desired people from the new database into your main database.

If you import a GEDCOM file that contains data that RootsMagic does not know how to handle, it will be put into what is called a "listing file". The listing file has the same name as the GEDCOM file, except that the file extension is .LST instead of .GED. The listing file is a plain text file that you can look at with the Windows notepad or any other text editor. It will list any lines from the GEDCOM file that it didn't understand.

Creating a GEDCOM File

To create a GEDCOM file, click the "Export" button on the toolbar, or do **"File, Export GEDCOM"** from the main menu. RootsMagic will bring up an options dialog for the GEDCOM file you want to create. Select the options you want, then click OK.

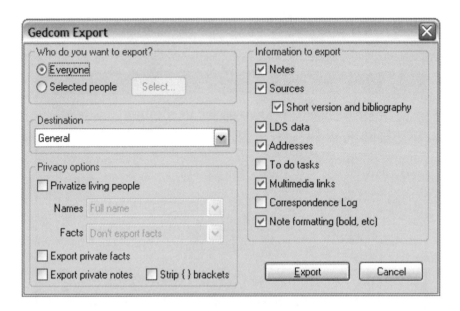

Who do you want to export? lets you tell RootsMagic whether you want to export everyone in your database, or to select exactly which people you want to export. If you choose **"Selected people"** RootsMagic will bring up a list of everybody in your database for you to select from. This selection list is the exact same screen described in the chapter titled "Custom Reports" (page 181). Simply select the individuals you want to include in the GEDCOM file.

Destination lets you tell RootsMagic what type of GEDCOM file you want to create.

➢ **General** - Use this option if you are creating the GEDCOM file to be read by anything other than the Ancestral File or TempleReady.

➢ **Ancestral File** - Use this option if you are creating the file to submit to the Ancestral File (a database maintained by the LDS Church).

➢ **TempleReady** - Use this option if you are creating the file to submit to TempleReady for name processing. You can also use the direct TempleReady commands described in the chapter titled LDS Support (page 250).

Privacy options lets you filter the way information is exported for living people. If you don't check this box, people will be exported whether they are living or not. If you do check this box, RootsMagic will use the two drop lists to determine exactly how to do the filtering.

➢ Names – Lets you choose whether to export the full name of living people, or whether to export the word "Living".

➢ Facts – Lets you select whether to export the full date and place for each fact, or to not export the fact at all. You can also choose from several other filtering options, like date only, year only, place only, and year and place.

☺ Tip

RootsMagic allows you to specify whether any particular fact type should be exported when creating a GEDCOM file (they are all exported by default). For example, if you want to create a GEDCOM file but not include Occupation facts, you can do **"Lists, Fact type list"** from the main menu, highlight **"Occupation"** in the list, click the **"Edit"** button, then uncheck the GEDCOM Export checkbox. RootsMagic will then ignore the Occupation facts for everyone when creating a GEDCOM file (until you edit the fact type again and check the GEDCOM Export checkbox).

This is especially useful if you want to get rid of all instances of a fact in your database. For example, lets say you want to get rid of all Ancestral File Numbers in your database. Turn off the Ancestral File Number fact (as described above), then export your database to a GEDCOM file. Then create a new (blank) database and import that GEDCOM file into the new database. You now have the same database minus the Ancestral File Numbers. This works just as well on any other fact type.

"Export private facts" lets you choose whether RootsMagic should include any facts (birth, marriage, death, etc.) that you have marked as "private".

"Export private notes" and **"Strip brackets"** let you choose whether RootsMagic should export any private notes you have entered. Private notes are described in more detail on page 74.

Information to export allows you to specify what types of data to export for each person.

- ➢ **Notes** - Check this box if you want notes included in the file.
- ➢ **Sources** - Check this box if you want sources and citations included in the file. You also have the option whether to export the short version and bibliography for each source (since most other programs do not support those features).
- ➢ **LDS data** – Check this box if you want to export LDS information like LDS baptisms, endowments, and sealings.
- ➢ **Addresses** - Check this box if you want current addresses included in the file. If you are sending the GEDCOM file to someone else, you probably don't want to include the addresses of all your relatives.
- ➢ **To do tasks** - Check this box if you want your to do items to be exported.
- ➢ **Multimedia links** - Check this box if you want the links to your photos and other scrapbook items to be exported. This does **not** export the photos themselves, just the link information.
- ➢ **Correspondence log** - Check this box if you want your correspondence log to be exported. Since the correspondence log is not part of the official GEDCOM standard, this option is primarily useful when creating a GEDCOM file to be imported back into RootsMagic.
- ➢ **Note formatting** – Check this box if you want RootsMagic to export the bold, italic, and underlining in your notes. Most other genealogy programs can't handle the formatting codes, but this allows you to preserve the formatting when the GEDCOM file will be imported back into RootsMagic.

After you select your options and click OK, RootsMagic will bring up the standard Windows file save dialog where you can enter the name you want to give your GEDCOM file.

Also, while GEDCOM is a very flexible file format, most programs implement it a little differently. Most of this has to do with the types and amount of data each program is capable of storing. If you create a GEDCOM file from RootsMagic and import it into another program which isn't as powerful as RootsMagic, you may lose a lot of your information simply because the other program has no place to store the information.

> ☺ **Tip**
>
> If you are transferring your full database back and forth between two computers (for example your desktop and a laptop), it is better to use the "File, Backup" command and "File, Restore" command which will not have any data loss associated with the GEDCOM format.

Should I Send GEDCOM Files by Email?

One of the most commonly asked questions about GEDCOM files is "How can I send a GEDCOM file by email so that the other person can use it" (or vice-versa). Unfortunately, every Internet provider is different, and so is every email package, so there is no easy answer.

The best way to email a GEDCOM to someone, is by sending it as an "attachment". An "attachment" is a way to attach a file (either text or binary) to the email, but it is **not** a part of the email text itself. Although GEDCOM files are basically text files, they have special formatting and can get quite large, and therefore shouldn't be sent as part of the email text itself (in other words, don't paste a GEDCOM into the message part of an email).

Since some email providers don't allow attachments to email messages, this fact alone eliminates those services from being able to dependably send or receive a GEDCOM file.

But (and there is always a "but"), just because an Internet provider can send and receive attachments, doesn't mean that it will work flawlessly. Some Internet providers "encode" attachments when they are sent out (and "decode" them when they are received). If you look at a GEDCOM file you have received, and it looks like total gibberish, then the file has probably been encoded (you may see terms like "MIME", "UUENCODED", etc).

Other systems don't support encoding and decoding, so they will just save the gibberish file, and expect that you will manually decode the file. If this is the case, you can use a program like WinZip (available at www.winzip.com) to decode the file for you.

Another problem you may encounter is the Internet provider breaking the file up into multiple pieces. In this case, you have to know what order the pieces go, and put them back together, and then you may still have to decode the file… what a headache. **Anyways, the bottom line is**… if you and the other person can easily send and receive attachments to email messages, then go for it. It doesn't hurt to try sending the file once or twice just to see if it will work. If it doesn't work though, just create the GEDCOM file on a floppy disk and send it by snail mail (US postal service). By the time you fiddle around with all your settings, the disk will have already made its way there.

Merging Duplicate Records

Two heads are not better than one.

Sometime you may find that you have the same person entered more than once in the same database. This is especially common after importing a GEDCOM file into an existing database.

RootsMagic helps you clean up these duplicate records by providing a "merge" capability. Merging lets you combine two records for a person into a single record.

RootsMagic allows you to manually merge duplicate records (one at a time), or it can search for duplicates for you. In addition, it also provides a number of different automatic merge options.

> **⚫ Warning**
>
> RootsMagic will always ask if you want to make a backup before doing a merge. You should always make a backup before a session of merging, so that if you accidentally merge the wrong records, you can restore your database from a backup.

Manual Merge

 To merge duplicate records one at a time, highlight one of the duplicate records on the main screen, then select **"Tools, Merge, Manual merge"** from the main menu, or click the right mouse button and choose "Merge" from the popup menu. RootsMagic will open the manual merge dialog.

Before you can merge records, you must select the records you want to merge. The merge screen will display the two records side by side, including names, sex, facts, and all immediate family members. The person who was highlighted on the main screen will already be selected on the left side of the dialog (the "primary" record).

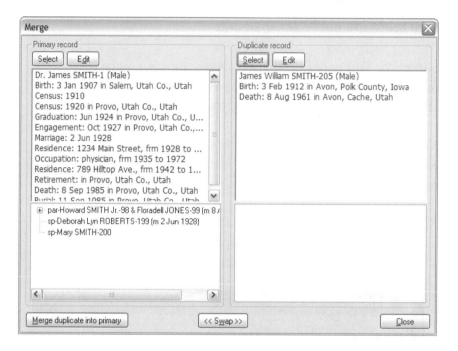

Click the **"Select"** button on the right side and RootsMagic will bring up the search screen for you to select the duplicate record. This search screen is exactly the same as the one described in the chapter titled "Finding People in Your Database" (page 60). Select the person, and his or her data will be displayed on the right half of the merge screen.

If you want to switch the position of the two records, simply click the **"<< Swap >>"** button before performing the merge.

When you are sure you want to merge the two records together, click the **"Merge duplicate into primary"** button. RootsMagic will copy all of the information (including family links, facts, notes, and sources) from the record on the right to the record on the left. If both records contain facts that are identical, RootsMagic will not duplicate the fact in the resulting merged person. RootsMagic will then delete the record on the right.

Duplicate Search and Merge

Although the Individual Merge is handy at times, it can also be tedious to search for the duplicate records one at a time.

RootsMagic can do a "duplicate search", which means it analyzes your database, and tries to find records that it thinks might be duplicates. It compares the names of the individuals in your database and finds individuals with closely matching names (the names don't have to be an exact match). These potential matches are then checked to make sure they are the same sex, and to check other information that you choose.

To do a duplicate search and merge, choose "Tools, Merge, Duplicate search / merge" from the main menu

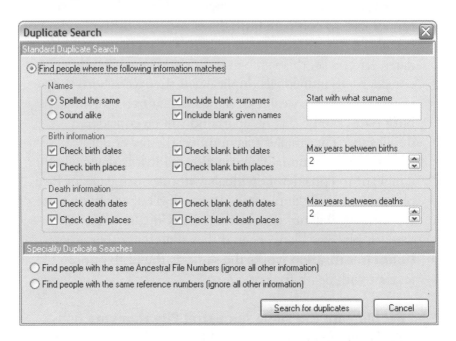

RootsMagic offers three different kinds of duplicate searches.

Find people where the following information matches lets you set options to have RootsMagic compare people using.

- ➤ **Names** lets you tell RootsMagic how people's names must match to be considered duplicates. You can specify whether matching names have to match exactly, or if they just need to sound alike. You can also choose whether blank names (both given and surnames) will be considered as matches with non blank names. Checking these boxes often leads to many false duplicates.

- ➤ **Starting surname** lets you tell RootsMagic where in the database to start the duplicate search. If you leave this blank, then RootsMagic will search the entire database for duplicates. If you enter "D", then RootsMagic will start with surnames beginning with the letter "D". If you enter "Jones", then RootsMagic will start with people with the last name "Jones".

- ➤ **Birth information** tells RootsMagic whether to compare birth information of people when checking for duplicates. You can choose to compare birth dates and / or birth places. You can also enter a maximum number of years between birth dates. If you set this value to 0, RootsMagic will only consider two individuals duplicates if they were born the exact same year. A value of 5 means that two individual's birth dates can be 5 years apart and still be considered duplicates. The smaller this number, the fewer duplicates RootsMagic will find. You can also tell RootsMagic whether you want to consider individuals without birth dates or birth places as possible duplicates. If you don't check these boxes, RootsMagic will not consider any individuals whose birth date (or place) is blank, even if they match in other ways.

- ➤ **Death information** works the same as the birth options (except with death data of course).

Find people with the same Ancestral File Numbers finds individuals with matching Ancestral File numbers. All other criteria are ignored.

Find people with the same reference numbers finds individuals with matching Reference numbers (REFN). All other criteria are ignored.

After you have made your choices and clicked the OK button, RootsMagic will search through your database for records that might be duplicates and display them in a list.

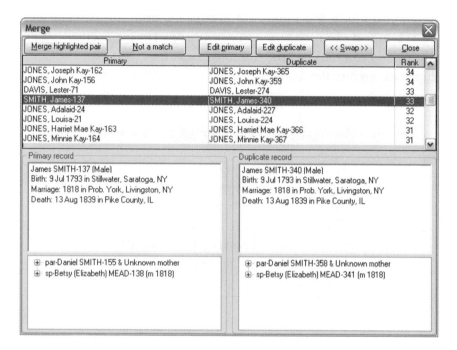

The list is sorted so that the most likely matches are at the top of the list. As you scroll down through the list of possible duplicates, the lower half of the dialog will display the full information about the two highlighted records.

If the two records on the row are duplicates, click the "Merge highlighted pair" button and RootsMagic will merge the two records.

If the two records on the row are NOT matches, you can click the "Not a match" button and RootsMagic will remove the pair from the merge list, and will not display them as matches in any future duplicate search / merges.

You can select "Tools, Merge, View 'not duplicates' list" from the menu to see a list of all pairs you have marked as not duplicates, and you can remove pairs from that list.

RootsMagic also provides buttons on the merge list to edit both the primary and duplicate records.

When you close the duplicate merge screen, RootsMagic will ask if you want to save your current position in the merge session. If you choose **"Yes"**, then the next time you do a duplicate merge, RootsMagic will let you continue merging where you left off.

> ☺ **Tip**
>
> When you merge duplicate records, you may find that the resulting record has two spouses, which happen to be the same person. This is because the spouse records are also duplicated. When you merge the duplicate spouse records, this situation will correct itself. **Don't** just delete the extra spouse, or you will end up with two families, one with an "unknown" spouse.

Automatic Merges

RootsMagic offers several automatic merge options when you select **"Tools, Merge, Automatic merges"** from the main menu. The following dialog box will appear where you can select any or all of the merges offered.

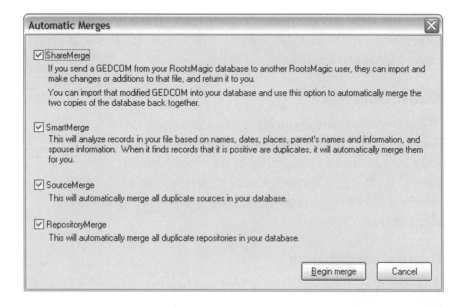

ShareMerge

This is one of the most useful merge options available if you intend to share data with family members who are also using RootsMagic. This option is explained in more detail in the following section "Collaborating With Family Members".

SmartMerge

SmartMerge will search for duplicates, and will assign a "score" to each pair of potential matching records based on: names, birth, christening, death, and burial, parent data, and marriage data. If the matching records "score" high enough, SmartMerge will automatically merge the records for you. Any conflicting data in any of the above fields will disqualify the records from being SmartMerged.

This is very useful as a first pass in doing a merge, then you can run the duplicate search and merge to pick up the duplicate records that automatic SmartMerge missed.

SmartMerge may reject records that appear to be exact duplicates, but this is usually because there is not enough information for SmartMerge to base its score on. In these cases, SmartMerge errs on the side of safety.

SourceMerge

This option will automatically merge all sources which are exact duplicates. If you select this option, you should also select the following option to merge duplicate repositories as well, since RootsMagic won't merge sources which are identical except for pointing to different repositories (even if the repositories are identical).

RepositoryMerge

There may be times when you find duplicate repositories in your database. Unfortunately, you can't just delete the duplicates because it will leave sources without their repository. This option will automatically merge all exactly duplicate repositories.

Collaborating With Family Members

One of the biggest problems facing families doing genealogy, is how to share their data back and forth without having to resort to long merge sessions.

Even when multiple family members start with the same original database, they may each enter different people, or make modifications to the same person. Then when you try to consolidate that information, you must either sit through a long merge session, or evaluate each database, picking and choosing which data is different and which is the same. RootsMagic offers several features that greatly simplify this process.

> **Warning**
>
> Both users need to be using RootsMagic for this feature to work. If one user is using a different program, it may throw away the unique ID number required for this feature.

Globally Unique ID – Any time you create a new person in RootsMagic, that person will be assigned a "hidden" ID number, which is unique to that person. This number is unique to that person… no other person (in any database) will ever receive that same unique ID number. If you export your database to a GEDCOM file, that unique ID number will travel with that person. And when you import that GEDCOM file into a RootsMagic database, that unique ID will come in with the person.

So what does this mean to me? Let's say you have a "master" database that you would like to share with family members. Simply create a GEDCOM file of your data and send it to them. When they import that GEDCOM file into their copy of RootsMagic, each person will have the same "unique ID" as the corresponding person in your master database.

You can now add, edit, or make other changes to people in your database, and they can do the same in their database. It is not necessary to keep the two databases "in sync".

I can already hear you asking *"how will we ever get those two databases combined into a single complete database"*?

Simple, just have your family member send you a GEDCOM file of their database, and import it into your database (remember… only do this if you are *both* using RootsMagic). At this point you will have a large number of duplicates, some of which are identical, and others that may differ a little bit. But RootsMagic knows which people are *really* the same, since their "unique ID" traveled with them.

So... select **"Tools, Merge, Automatic merges"** from the main menu, and leave all four options selected. RootsMagic will automatically merge the duplicate repositories and sources that exist. Then it will automatically merge everybody in the database who has the same unique ID. If there is conflicting information in the two people's data, RootsMagic will keep both copies of that data. For example, if the birth date of a person was changed in one of the databases, RootsMagic will keep both birth facts for the person.

Research Aids

Research is the process of going up alleys to see if they are blind.
—Marston Bates

Although RootsMagic is primarily intended to store information you have already collected, it can also assist you in your research.

To Do List

The to-do list (sometimes called a research log) provides a place to save all those research tasks you need to accomplish. It lets you enter an unlimited number of "tasks" for each person or family. You can even enter general to-do tasks which are not specific to a single person.

You can access a person's to do list from the main screen by highlighting that person, then clicking the "todo" button on the toolbar, then selecting "Person", or selecting **"Edit, To do, Person"** from the main menu. You can also access the to-do list from a person's edit screen by clicking the **"To Do"** tab on that screen.

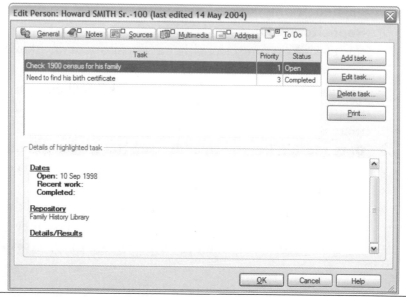

Add task lets you add a new task to the list. The following dialog will appear where you can enter the task information.

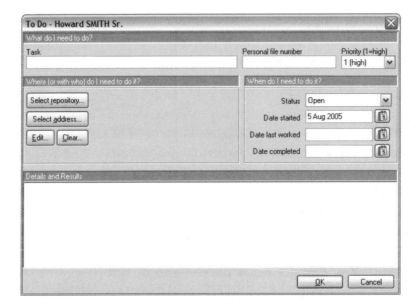

> **Task** is a one-line description of the task.
> **Personal file number** lets you enter a number or text to tie this todo item to your paper records.
> **Priority** lets you specify how urgent this task is from 1 (highest priority) through 9 (lowest)
> **Repository/Address** is the place where you need to do this task. You can select either a repository or an address, as well as edit the location or clear it.
> **Status** lets you specify whether the task is still open or whether it has been completed. You can also denote if there is a problem with the task.
> **Date started** lets you enter the date you created this task.
> **Date of most recent work** lets you enter the most recent date you worked on this task.
> **Date completed** lets you enter the date you finished this task. Although many people will just delete a task they have finished, others want to keep a record of the tasks.

➤ **Details and results** allows you to enter full details on the task, what needs to be accomplished, and what the results were.

Edit task lets you modify the highlighted task in the list. You can also double click a task in the list to edit the task.

Delete task will delete the highlighted task from the list. This is useful when you have completed the task and no longer need it.

Print will let you print the "to do" list for the current person.

You can enter and edit todo tasks for a family in much the same way as you do for people. Just click the "Todo" tab on the Edit Family dialog to bring up the same screen for the family.

RootsMagic also has a "master todo list" which lets you view all the todo items in the database, and allows you to enter "general" todo tasks which aren't tied to a specific person or family. To access the master todo list, do "Lists, Todo list" from the main menu. You can add "New" todo tasks, "Edit" any todo task, "Delete" a todo task, or "Print" the todo list from here.

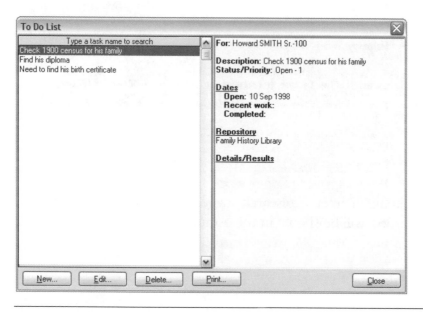

GenSmarts Integration

 GenSmarts is an add-on program which can make research suggestions for individuals in your database. Although GenSmarts is normally run as a standalone program, RootsMagic has integrated direct support for it.

If you have GenSmarts installed, all you have to do is highlight a person on the main RootsMagic screen and select "Tools, GenSmarts suggestions" from the menu. You can also customize the toolbar to add a GenSmarts button which can be clicked (customizing the toolbar is described on page 15).

RootsMagic will automatically request research suggestions from GenSmarts and will display this dialog.

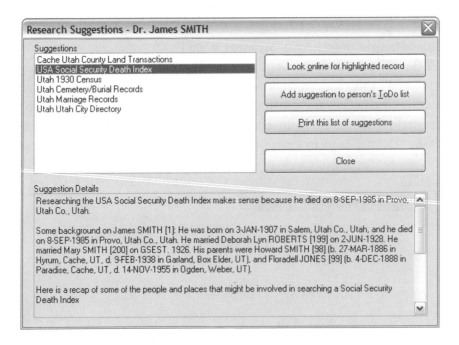

As you highlight each research suggestion, details about that suggestion will be shown in the bottom half of the dialog.

If the highlighted record type is available online, you can click the "Look online for highlighted record" button and RootsMagic will do an online search for the person in that record.

You can click the "Add suggestion to person's ToDo list" button to (what else?) add the suggestion to the person's todo list. This lets you keep track of any progress you have made on that suggestion.

And finally, you can print the list of suggestions (along with all the details for each suggestion).

Note

If you don't own GenSmarts, you can order it directly from RootsMagic at www.rootsmagic.com. You can also download a free trial version as well.

Correspondence List

The Correspondence List is designed to help you keep track of all your genealogy related correspondence. The list does not provide the capability to write the letter itself. That is for your word processor or good old pen and pencil. What it does do is provide a location to enter information about letters and packages you send (and receive), so that you can easily see whether you ever wrote that letter you meant to send.

To access the correspondence list, select "Lists, Correspondence list" from the main menu.

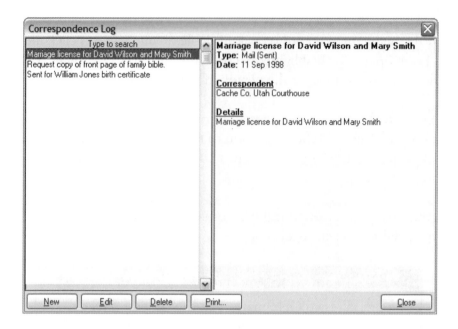

To add an item to the correspondence list, click the "New" button and RootsMagic will display the following dialog.

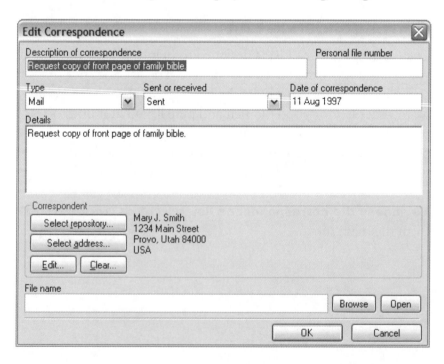

➢ **Description of correspondence** – A brief description of the correspondence that is displayed in the correspondence list.

➢ **Personal file number** – Allows you to enter a number which ties this entry to your hard copies.

➢ **Type** – Lets you specify the type of correspondence: mail, email, telephone, fax, or other.

➢ **Sent or received** – Lets you specify whether you sent the correspondence or received it from someone else.

➢ **Date of correspondence** – Enter the date you mailed or received your letter or package.

➢ **Details** – Enter details about why you wrote, or what the received correspondence was about.

➢ **Correspondent** – Lets you enter the person or organization you corresponded with. You can select either a repository or an address. You can also edit the correspondent information or clear it altogether.

➢ **File name** – Lets you enter a file name for the correspondence. This is useful if you wrote a letter in your word processor and want to be able to access it from RootsMagic. You can click the "Browse" button to select the file with the file dialog. If you click the "Open" button, RootsMagic will open the file using whatever program it is associated with in Windows.

To edit an item in the correspondence list, highlight the item in the list, and click the **"Edit"** button. RootsMagic will display the same dialog used when you added the item. Make any desired changes and click the **OK** button.

To delete an item in the correspondence list, highlight the item in the list, and click the **"Delete"** button. RootsMagic will ask if you are sure you want to delete the item.

To print the correspondence list, click the **"Print"** button. RootsMagic will allow you to print the correspondence as described on page 126.

Blank forms

RootsMagic will print a number of blank forms designed to help you with your research, including:

➤ Blank pedigree charts
➤ Blank family group sheets
➤ Cemetery Records Form
➤ Correspondence Log
➤ Research Log

These forms can be found under the **"Blank Forms"** section of the Reports dialog.

Sending Books to Family Members

One of the best ways to collect information from family members is to send them a book of your family and ask them to provide any missing information. Simply include a letter with a copy of the book specifying what information you want for each person.

As an alternative (albeit a labor intensive one), you can add facts to people and enter a sequence of underline characters where unknown dates or places would go. When you print a book with underlines like this, the sentences will read like:

He was born _____ in _____.

and your relatives can simply fill in the blanks. Make sure you offer to send a copy of the completed book if they reply with additional information.

Other Printouts

RootsMagic also provides several other printouts that can be helpful in your research. These particular printouts can be found under the "Lists" section of the Reports dialog.

The **Fact list** allows you to generate lists of any facts you are missing or have duplicated. For example, you can print out a list of every person who is missing a birth fact, or any person you have multiple death facts for. In addition, it is also useful for determining what information you have entered into RootsMagic that you do not have any documentation for.

The **Individual list** will help you track down those end-of-line individuals that you need to research to take your family line back further.

The **Problem list** will point out potential data errors, such as people being born after their mother died. While many of these are data entry errors, some of them may be erroneous data that you typed in correctly.

The **Missing Information list** lets you print a list of people who are missing any fact or facts. You can even find people who are just missing a date or place for a fact. RootsMagic will leave a blank on the list so you can use the list as a worksheet to find the information.

The **Surname Statistics list** will create a list of all surnames in your database, how many times each surname occurs, and the earliest and most recent year the surname occurs.

The **LDS Ordinance list** is useful if you are a member of the LDS Church and need to know which people have not had their ordinances completed.

Creating a Family Website

One of the best ways to find out more about your family is to get in contact with other people who are researching the same information. In the past, this required writing a lot of letters and making a lot of phone calls. With the advent of the Internet and the World Wide Web, it is becoming easier to make contact with other researchers, if you can let them know of your research interests.

RootsMagic can help you with this by helping you create a website with your genealogical information, and links where other researchers can email you if they have any common information. You can learn how to create a family website by reading the chapter titled, "Putting Your Family on the Web" (page 236).

Keeping a Research Database

When doing your research, you will sometimes come across individuals who might be a part of your family line, but you aren't sure and can't prove anything yet.

One way to keep track of these individuals is to create a new database called RESEARCH. When you come across unproven ancestors, enter them in the research database the same way you enter your family into your main database.

Entering your unproven ancestors into RootsMagic allows you to maintain unproven family lines, facts, and documentation on each of these people, but by keeping these individuals in a separate database, you eliminate the problem of removing them if they turn out to be unrelated.

Then, when you prove that these folks really are part of your family, you can drag and drop them into your main database.

Tools

If the only tool you have is a hammer, you tend to see every problem as a nail. - Abraham Maslow

RootsMagic provides a large number of tools that make managing your data easier.

Problem Search

When entering information into any program there is the possibility of making a mistake. RootsMagic's problem search is designed to help you find these mistakes.

To search for potential problems, do **"Tools, Problem search, Problem list"** from the menu, tell RootsMagic which problems you want it to search for, and it will generate a list of any person who has one of the selected problems.

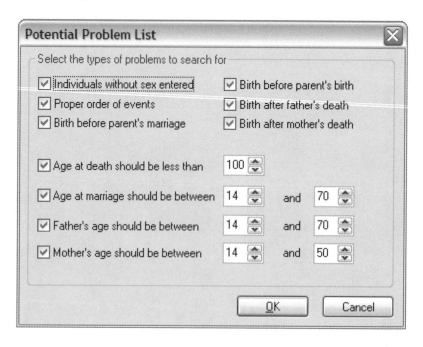

"Individuals without sex entered" will find individuals who have "Unknown" entered for their sex.

"Proper order of events" will catch problems like a person getting married before their birth or after their death.

"Birth before parent's marriage" will list individuals whose birth date falls before their parent's marriage date.

"Birth before parent's birth" will list individuals whose birth date is earlier than their mother's or father's birth date.

"Birth after father's death" will list individuals whose birth date is after their father's death date.

"Birth after mother's death" will list individuals whose birth date is after their mother's death date.

"Age at death should be less than X" will list individuals whose age at death is greater than the value you enter.

"Age at marriage should be between X and Y" will list individuals whose age at marriage is outside the range you enter.

"Father's age should be between X and Y" will list individuals whose father's age was outside the range you enter when the person was born.

"Mother's age should be between X and Y" will list individuals whose mother's age was outside the range you enter when the person was born.

Once you click OK, RootsMagic will display a list of potential problems which looks like this.

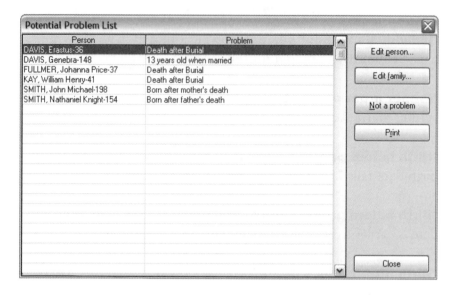

RootsMagic allows you to edit either the person or the family, because some problems involve editing the person's information, while other problems involve editing the data for another person in the family. If you double click on a problem in the list, RootsMagic will detect whether you need to edit the person or family and will automatically open the proper edit screen.

If a problem in the list isn't really a problem (for example if Aunt Mary really was 102 years old), you can highlight the non-problem and click the "Not a problem" button. RootsMagic will remove the item from the list and will not display it as a problem the next time you run the problem search.

If you ever want to see what "problems" RootsMagic is ignoring, you can do "Tools, Problem search, View 'not a problem' list". You can remove items from that list so that the problem search will detect them once again.

If you want to print the problem list, simply click the "Print" button on the dialog.

Setting the Living Flag

When you import a GEDCOM file you may often have individuals with no birth or death dates, or other means for RootsMagic to know how to apply the "Living" flag for the person.

The "Set Living" function lets you set (or clear) the living flag for any group of people in your database. Select **"Tools, Set living"** from the main menu and RootsMagic will bring up a dialog asking if you want to set the living flag to true or false for a group of people. Choose the desired setting and click OK. RootsMagic will then bring up the selection screen (page 181) for you to choose the individuals whose living flag you want to change.

Setting Relationships to a Person

RootsMagic can display relationships of the highlighted person in the status line at the bottom of the screen. You can choose which person to base these relationships on. Select "Tools, Set relationships" from the menu and RootsMagic will bring up the following dialog.

RootsMagic will default to the currently highlighted person, but you can click "Change" to select a different person. Click "Set relationships" to set the relationships to that person.

From that point on (until you change it), RootsMagic will display the relationship of the highlighted person on the main screen to that person. For example, if you set relationships for yourself, then when your 3rd great grandfather is highlighted, the status line will display "third great grandfather".

Color Coding People

Have you ever wanted to be able to quickly tell whether a person in your database is part of a particular group? RootsMagic makes this easy by letting you color code any group of people. Selecting "Tools, Color code people" from the main menu and RootsMagic will bring up the following dialog.

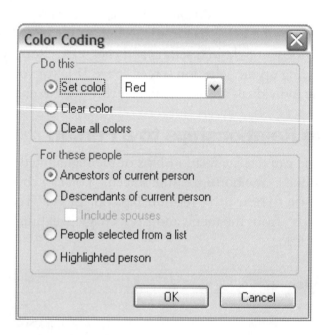

You can set or clear the display color for any group of people.

> **Set color** – Lets you choose the color to set for a group of people. You can select from 16 different color code groups.
> **Clear color** – Lets you clear the color for any group of people
> **Clear all colors** – Lets you clear (reset) the color for the entire database

You can perform these operations for:

> Ancestors of the current person
> Descendants of the current person. You can also choose whether to include the spouses of descendants.
> People selected from a list. If you choose this option, RootsMagic will bring up the selection screen (page 181) for you to choose the individuals whose living flag you want to change.
> The currently highlighted person on the screen.

When you set the color for a group of people, it sets the color for people matching those characteristics at that instant. If you later add or edit people you may need to re-run the color coding.

The Date Calculator

The date calculator lets you calculate dates and the amount of time between dates. Selecting **"Tools, Date calculator"** from the main menu will bring up the date calculator. The date calculator can also be brought up when you are entering dates for facts (like birth, death, etc.).

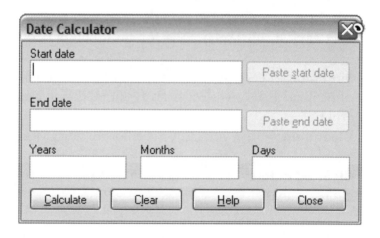

The "Calculate" button calculates differently depending on which fields you have filled out.

If you fill out...	Calculate will determine...
Start date and Years, Months, Days	End date
End date and Years, Months, Days	Start date
Start date and End date	Years, months, and days

When you are using the date calculator while entering facts for a person, it contains 2 additional buttons labeled "Paste start date" and "Paste end date". Clicking on these buttons will copy either the start date or the end date into the fact's date field, and will then close the date calculator. Clicking the "Clear" button simply erases all the fields in the date calculator so you can do another calculation.

 Tip

The date calculator is the perfect tool for determining an approximate birth date from a tombstone inscription like "Died 12 March 1942 at the age of 82 Years, 10 Months, and 2 Days".

The Relationship Calculator

If you have ever wondered how you are related to another person in your database, the relationship calculator is the quickest way to find out. Simply do **"Tools, Relationship calculator"** from the main menu.

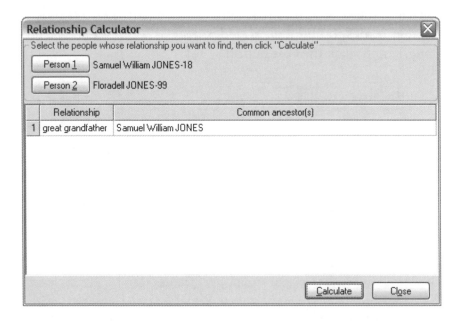

You must first select the 2 individuals whose relationship you want to know. Person 1 will already contain the name of the person who was highlighted on the main screen. Click on the **"Person 2"** button and select the other individual. Finally, click the **"Calculate"** button and RootsMagic will tell you how the two people are related, and who the common ancestors are.

> ☺ **Tip**
>
> If you want a chart that shows the relationship between two people, check out the Relationship Chart described on page 152. RootsMagic also provides a supercharged version of the Relationship Calculator called the Kinship List. The Kinship List will print out every relative of a person and list their relationship to that person.

The Soundex Calculator

The Soundex calculator simply calculates the Soundex code for any name you type into it.

To access the Soundex calculator, select "Tools, Soundex calculator" from the main menu. There are no buttons to click; it calculates the code as you type it in. You can backspace and type in other names to find their Soundex code as well. When you are done, simply click the **Close** button.

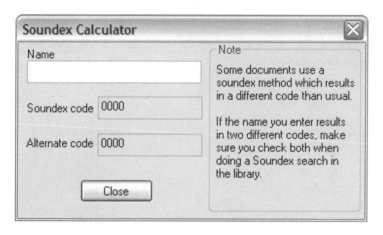

Many census and other types of records use the Soundex method to group similar sounding names together. For example, "Smith" and "Smythe" both have the same Soundex code "S530", so grouping by Soundex would keep all the Smiths and Smythes together.

> ✎ **Note**
>
> Some genealogical records (most notably census records) use a slightly modified algorithm when calculating the Soundex code. Although only a few names actually end up with different codes, RootsMagic supports both algorithms. If RootsMagic calculates two different Soundex codes, make sure you check under both codes.

Spell Checking

RootsMagic provides a built-in spell checker, and includes the ability to add your own words to its dictionary (which is especially important for family names).

To spell check the text in a single note, click the spell check button on the note editor toolbar, or click the right mouse button in the note editor and select Spell Check from the menu, or press F7 while the cursor is in the note field. RootsMagic will begin spell checking the note text.

To spell check all the notes in your database at once, select "Tools, Spell check" from the main menu. RootsMagic will display the following dialog and allow you to check individual notes, family notes, and fact notes (in any combination).

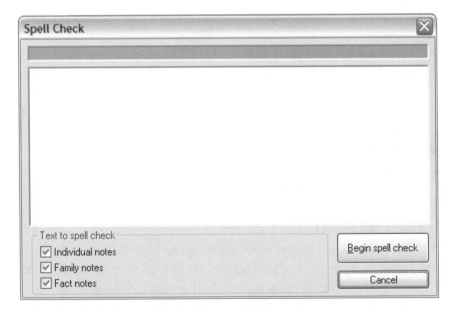

Select the types of notes you want to spell check, then click OK. RootsMagic will begin checking the notes in your database.

When an unknown word is found, RootsMagic will display the Spell Check dialog with the unknown word. You can type in the correct spelling, or you can select one of the suggested replacements from the Suggestions list.

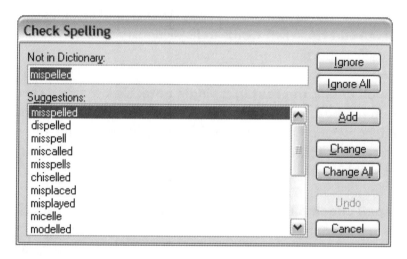

> **Ignore** – Causes this occurrence of the misspelled word to be skipped. If the same misspelled word appears later, it will be reported.

> **Ignore All** – Causes this and all further occurrences of the misspelled word to be skipped. You might use this button if the word reported as a misspelling is actually spelled correctly. If the word is one you use frequently, you may wish to ignore it permanently by selecting the **Add** button.

> **Add** – Causes the reported word to be added to the dictionary. Use the **Add** button if a correctly spelled word you use often is reported as a misspelling (e.g., your family name). If the word is not used frequently, you may want to select the **Ignore** or **Ignore All** buttons instead.

> **Change** – Causes the reported word to be replaced with the highlighted word in the Suggestions list. Only this occurrence of the reported word is replaced. If you want this and all following occurrences of the word replaced, select the **Change All** button. If the **Change To** box is empty, the **Change** button changes to **Delete**.

> **Change All** – Causes this and all following occurrences of the reported word to be replaced with the highlighted word in the

Suggestions list. If you want only this occurrence of the word to be replaced, use the **Change** button.

➤ **Cancel** – Exits from the spell check dialog without making any more changes.

Search and Replace

Probably the most powerful data manipulation feature in RootsMagic (and possibly the most dangerous to your data if used improperly) is global search and replace. **To do a global search and replace**, select "Search, Search and replace" from the main menu. RootsMagic will display the following dialog.

RootsMagic doesn't simply search and replace any and every piece of data. You must tell it what type of data you want to search and replace by selecting from the "Search in" drop list. You can search and replace in:

Names – Given
Names – Surnames
Names – Nicknames
Names – Prefix
Names – Suffix
Places
Multimedia filenames
Notes – General
Notes – Family
Notes – Facts

Sources – Footnote
Sources – Short version
Sources – Bibliography
Sources – Name in list
Sources – Actual text
Sources – Comments
Citations – Page number
Citations – Actual text
Citations - Comments

Then just type in the text you want to search for, and the text you want to replace it with, and click **OK**. RootsMagic will bring up each item to replace one at a time for you to confirm. You can **"Replace"** or **"Skip"** the item and go onto the next item, or you can **"Replace all"** items without confirmation.

Search and replace can also be used as "Search and Delete" by just leaving the **"Replace with"** field blank. RootsMagic will then search for each occurrence of the text you enter, and replace it with nothing (thus deleting it). Be careful with this new knowledge.

☺ **Tip**

If you ever move your linked photos to another directory, you will learn that RootsMagic can't find your pictures anymore (since RootsMagic just stores the pathname to the pictures). Searching and replacing the multimedia filename is a great way to solve this problem.

Lets say your photos were originally in:

C:\RMAGIC\PHOTOS\

but you moved them all to:

D:\ROOTSMAGIC\PICTURES\

All you need to do is globally search the multimedia filenames for C:\RMAGIC\PHOTOS\ and replace it with D:\ROOTSMAGIC\PICTURES\

Count Trees In Database

The "Count trees" command simply counts the number of trees in your database. This is especially useful if you have imported

GEDCOM files into your database. Often those GEDCOM files may contain multiple unlinked trees that you are unaware of.

To generate a list of the trees in your database, select "Tools, Count trees in database" from the main menu. RootsMagic will count the number of trees and display them in a list.

The list will list each tree in your database, along with the name and record number of one person in each tree to help you find the tree in your database.

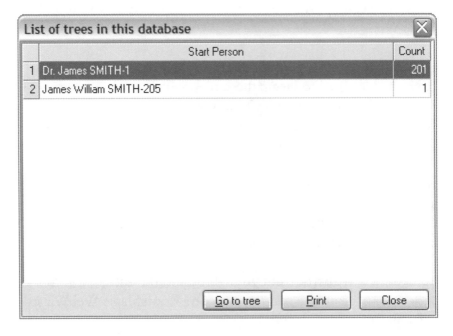

You can print the list by clicking the "Print" button, or you can bring a tree up on the main screen by highlighting the tree in the list and clicking the "Go to tree" button.

Putting Your Family on the Web
Oh what a tangled web we weave...

Creating a Family Website

With the advent of the Internet and the World Wide Web, it is becoming easier to make contact with family members and other researchers. Many people now have Internet accounts, and a most of these accounts include free "server" space with the account. Server space is simply an area on another computer where you can upload files that can be displayed on the World Wide Web.

Unfortunately, most people who have this free server space don't have any idea how to create these files, which need to be in a format called HTML (HyperText Markup Language). RootsMagic gets around this problem by providing an automatic website creator built right into the program.

RootsMagic will create all the files necessary for your website, and will place those files together in a directory on your hard drive. Your website can include: notes, sources, photographs, email link, surname index, and a bibliography.

To create a website from your RootsMagic data, select "Internet, Create a web site" from the main menu. The RootsMagic WebWizard will appear.

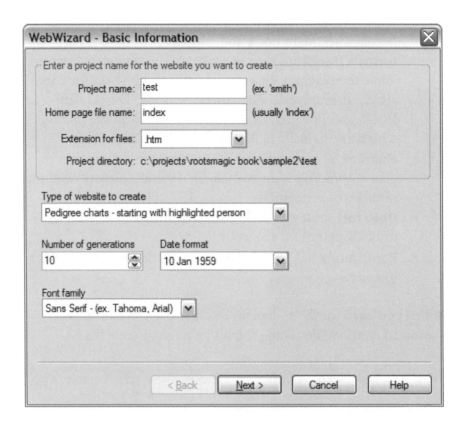

The first screen of the wizard asks you for basic information for your website.

> **Project name** is the name of your "project". RootsMagic will use this name to create a subdirectory under your data directory to hold all the project files.

> **Home page file name** lets you select the "starting" file for your web site. Usually you should set this to "index", especially if you plan to upload your web site to the RootsMagic server.

> **Extension for files** lets you specify whether you want the file extensions for your files to be .htm or .html. Usually you will just pick .htm, but some internet servers require the use of .html.

> **Type of website to create** lets you select the general format for your web site. RootsMagic offers a wide variety of formats, including family group sheet, pedigree

chart, pedigree chart with group sheet combo, ancestor book, descendant book and alphabetical book. The book formats print your data in a narrative (sentence) structure, while the pedigree chart and family group sheet formats are more graphical. The Ancestor Book, Descendant Book, and Pedigree Chart formats start with the person who was originally highlighted on the main screen.

➢ **Number of generations** lets you specify the number of generations you want to include. Not all formats need the number of generations.

➢ **Date format** lets you choose what format you want dates to be displayed on the website.

➢ **Font family** lets you choose the style of font used in your website.

When you have finished filling in the first page, click the **"Next"** button to continue designing the home page of your site.

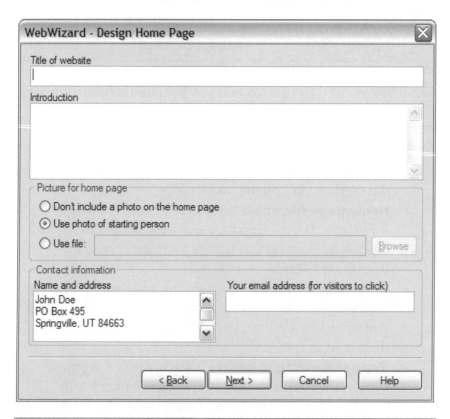

- ➤ **Title of website** lets you specify the text that is displayed at the top of your home page.
- ➤ **Introduction** is a brief paragraph or two where you can tell visitors about your family, research, surnames, or any other information. This provides an opportunity for you to enter a few lines explaining your purpose for creating the website, or a few details about the starting person for this website. For example, you might write something like "This site contains the descendants of Jeremiah Johnson. Jeremiah was one of the original settlers of Johnson County back in 1823".
- ➤ **Don't include a photo on the home page** tells RootsMagic not to put any photograph on the home page.
- ➤ **Use photo of starting person** tells RootsMagic to include a photo of the person who was originally highlighted. Not all website types have a starting person, so sometimes this option isn't available.
- ➤ **Use file** lets you select any photo whether it is being used by RootsMagic or not. Click the Browse button to select a photo off your hard drive.
- ➤ **Contact information** allows you to enter a physical address and email address where visitors to your site can contact you. RootsMagic will place these addresses on your home page, and will even turn your email address into a link that visitors can click on to send you email.

When you are happy with your choices, click the "Next" button to continue. You can also click the "Back" button to move back to the previous screen in case you need to change something there.

The next screen asks you to select the visual appearance of the website. You can select the various colors or background textures for the site, as well as choosing whether you want a "navigation bar".

The Navigation bar is a small part of the screen which has navigation links to the various pages in your site. You can have the navigation bar on the left side of the screen (which is the default), or on the screen top, or bottom, or top and bottom. You can even choose not to have a navigation bar at all.

The Advanced HTML button lets you enter pure HTML code that will be placed at the top and bottom of each page that RootsMagic generates. Be careful with this feature. While it is powerful, you can make a mess of your web pages if you don't know exactly what you are doing. But if you do mess up, just run the WebWizard again and remove anything you entered here and all will work again.

Colors lets you select the color for both the main screen and the navigation bar, as well as the text color in each. You can also choose the color of links, including the color when the user's cursor hovers over the link.

Background textures lets you choose background images for both the main screen and navigation bar. You can select any image off your hard drive. RootsMagic provides several nice textures which are fairly easy to read text on.

When you are happy with your selections, click the **"Next"** button to continue. You can also click the **"Back"** button to move back to the previous screen in case you need to change something there.

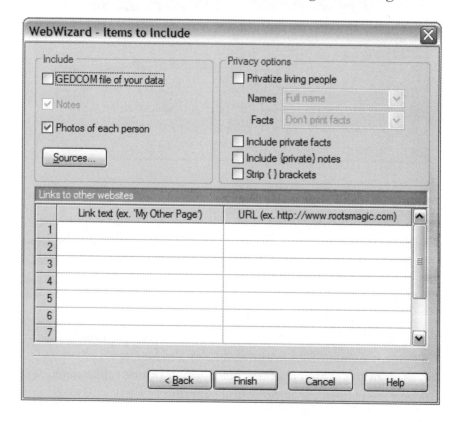

Sources - Lets you tell RootsMagic how to export sources for the website (if at all). It will bring up the source option dialog described on page 110.

Notes will include any notes you have entered for the person.

Photos of each person lets you include the photos of each person on your website. RootsMagic will use the primary photo you have attached to each person.

GEDCOM file of your data lets you tell RootsMagic to create a GEDCOM file of the names in your website. If you check this box, a GEDCOM file will be created and a link will be created on your home page where a person can click and download the GEDCOM file.

> ☺ **Tip**
>
> You may not want to include a GEDCOM file of your data, since a visitor with common ancestors may just download the GEDCOM and never contact you. You may want to put a note in the Introduction of your web site that says something like "If you find any information that we have in common, please send me an email and I will be happy to send you a GEDCOM file with my data".

Privacy options lets you "privatize" your website. If you don't check the "privatize living people" box, people's information will be included whether they are living or not. If you do check this box, RootsMagic will use the two drop lists to determine exactly how to do the filtering.

➤ Names – Lets you choose whether to display the full name of living people, or whether to display the word "Living".

➤ Facts – Lets you select whether to display the full date and place for each fact, or to not display the fact at all. You can also choose from several other filtering options, like date only, year only, place only, and year and place.

"Include private facts" lets you choose whether RootsMagic should include any facts (birth, marriage, death, etc.) that you have marked as "private".

"Print private notes" and **"Strip brackets"** let you choose whether RootsMagic should include any private notes you have entered. Private notes are described in more detail on page 74.

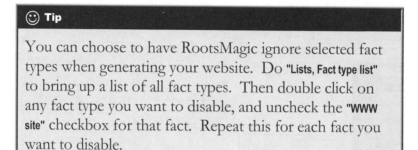

You can choose to have RootsMagic ignore selected fact types when generating your website. Do "Lists, Fact type list" to bring up a list of all fact types. Then double click on any fact type you want to disable, and uncheck the "WWW site" checkbox for that fact. Repeat this for each fact you want to disable.

Links to other websites lets you include up to 10 web site links on your home page. Just enter the URL and the text you want to display for the link. When you are ready to generate your website, click the "Finished" button and RootsMagic will create the web site files and then display the following screen.

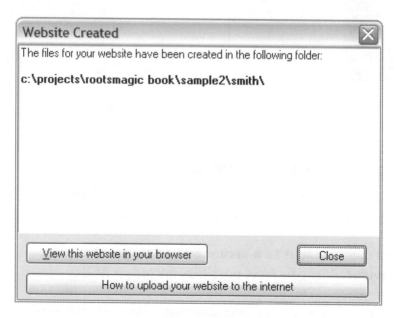

View this website in browser will bring up the website you just generated. This preview is just looking at the HTML files on your hard drive. They are not actually on the Internet until you upload them.

Here is an example of what a RootsMagic generated pedigree chart page looks like:

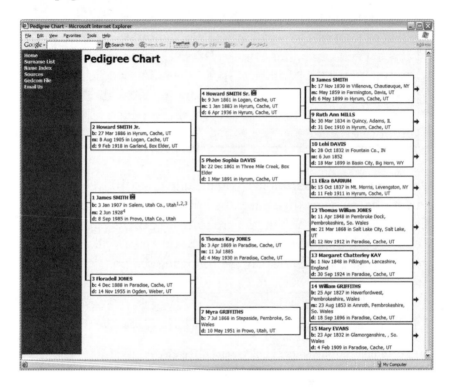

Uploading Your Website

Once RootsMagic has created the files for your family web site, you need to upload them to the Internet.

You can upload it to a server owned by your Internet provider. Many Internet providers (including AOL, CompuServe, etc) offer free server space with your Internet account. If you aren't sure if your provider offers free server space, call or send them an email. They can also provide you with the necessary software and information on uploading to their server. You can also get free server space for your website by visiting www.rootsweb.com.

To upload the website that RootsMagic creates, you will probably need an FTP program, which is software that copies files from your computer to the internet (and vice versa). There are a number of FTP programs available, but two of the most popular are CuteFTP (www.cuteftp.com) and WS_FTP (www.ipswitch.com).

☺ **Tip**

After you have uploaded your family website, you will want to register your website with the many search engines on the internet, such as AltaVista, Google and others. This will help others find your website when they use one of these search engines.

The Internet Menu

The "Internet" item on RootsMagic's main menu provides a number of capabilities which require Internet access.

- ➤ **Create a website** - Creates a website (HTML) from the information in your database (page 236).
- ➤ **RootsMagic.com** – Opens your browser to the rootsmagic.com website.
- ➤ **Message Boards** - Internet message boards covering RootsMagic and other subjects.
- ➤ **FAQ** – Opens your browser to the frequently asked questions area for RootsMagic.
- ➤ **Technical support** – Opens your browser to the technical support page for RootsMagic.
- ➤ **Family Reunion Planner** - Hundreds of ideas, tips, and resources for planning the perfect family reunion.

Other Internet Resources

There are a number of resources on the Internet to assist you when learning and using RootsMagic.

http://www.RootsMagic.com

This website provides information about RootsMagic, including:

- ➤ Message boards
- ➤ A list of RootsMagic user groups
- ➤ Frequently Asked Questions (FAQ)
- ➤ Program updates
- ➤ And more

ROOTSMAGIC-USERS mail list

This is an Internet mail list where you can get in contact with other RootsMagic users. To join the RootsMagic Users mail list, send email with the word subscribe in the body to:

ROOTSMAGIC-USERS-L-request@rootsweb.com

If you want to receive the mail list in "digest" format, send email with the word subscribe in the body to:

ROOTSMAGIC-USERS-D-request@rootsweb.com

LDS Support

Members of the LDS church have additional requirements which RootsMagic provides support for. These features are optional, and can be enabled or disabled by checking the **"LDS Support"** checkbox in the database options dialog (see page 264).

Entering Information

Although it is possible to enter LDS ordinances the same way as births, deaths, and other facts, RootsMagic provides an LDS ordinance template for each person in your database.

To bring up the LDS ordinance template, highlight the person on the main screen and select **"Edit, LDS ordinances"** from the main menu, or press **Ctrl+L**. If you are in the person's edit screen, you can also click the **"LDS Ordinances"** button on the edit dialog.

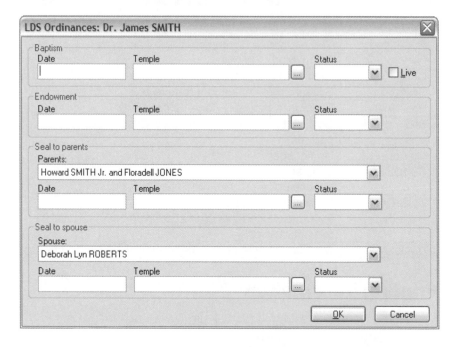

Simply fill in the blanks with the dates and temples for the baptism, endowment, sealing to parents, and sealing to spouse.

If the person has more than one spouse or set of parents entered, the drop lists in those sections can be used to switch between the other spouses or parents.

The baptism field has a checkbox which allows you to specify whether the baptism was done while the person was living (or whether it was done by proxy). Switching between live and proxy causes the place field and place list to switch between temples and places.

In addition to date and temple fields, each ordinance also has a status field, which support special LDS statuses. If you have a date and a temple for an ordinance, you should just leave the "Status" field blank (don't even use Completed, since that status means the work has been done but you don't know when or where). Below is the list of statuses which are available (some are only available in certain types of ordinances).

Status	What it means
Completed	The ordinance is finished but you don't know when or where.
Submitted	The ordinance is submitted and waiting for completion.
Child	Died before 8 years old
Stillborn	Stillborn (ordinances not required)
Pre-1970	Ordinance probably done before 1970
BIC	Born in the covenant (only used for sealing to parents)
Do not seal	Do not seal
Canceled	Ordinance canceled and considered invalid (seal to spouse only)
DNS/CAN	Do not seal / Canceled
Excluded	Patron excluded this ordinance from being cleared in this submission
Uncleared	Data for clearing ordinance request was insufficient

Printing Information

The LDS ordinance lists will print LDS ordinance information for the people in your database.

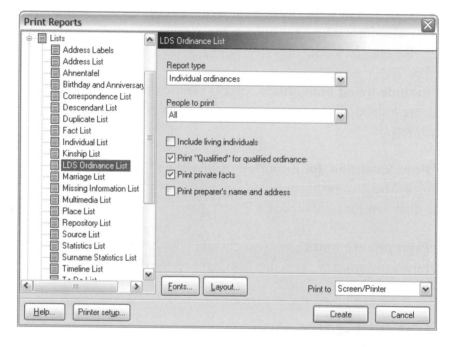

To print the LDS ordinance lists, click the Print button on the toolbar, or select **"File, Print"** from the main menu. Then select the list called **"LDS Ordinance List"**. RootsMagic will display the following dialog.

"Report type" lets you select which unfinished ordinance list to print.

➢ **Individual ordinances** - lists individuals and the dates for LDS baptism, endowment, and sealing to parents.
➢ **Marriage sealings** - lists families and the marriage date and sealing to spouse date.

"People to print" lets you select which individuals to include in the selected list.

➢ **All** – Everyone in the database
➢ **Only those missing ordinances** - prints only individuals who are missing at least one ordinance

- **Only those with all ordinances completed** - prints only individuals who are not missing any ordinances
- **Only those with "submitted" ordinances** - prints only individuals who have at least one ordinance with a status of "Submitted".
- **Only those with "qualified" ordinances** - prints only individuals who have at least one ordinance which is qualified for temple work.

"Include living individuals" gives you the option to ignore living individuals (since you can't do temple work for them anyways).

"Print 'qualified' for qualified ordinances" will cause RootsMagic to print the word "qualified" for any ordinance that is qualified for temple work.

"Print private facts" lets you choose whether RootsMagic should include any facts that you have marked as "private".

TempleReady

One goal of the LDS genealogist is to submit names for temple ordinances. In order to do that, a file must be created for submission to the TempleReady program.

 **To create a file for TempleReady submission**, select "File, TempleReady" from the main menu. RootsMagic will display the following dialog.

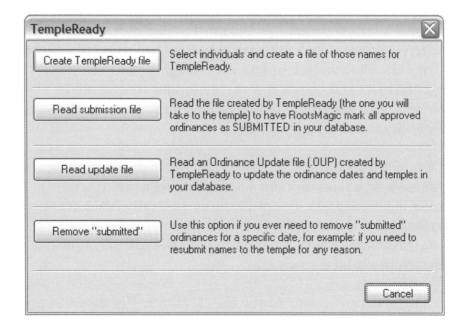

To create a file for TempleReady, click the "Create TempleReady file" button.

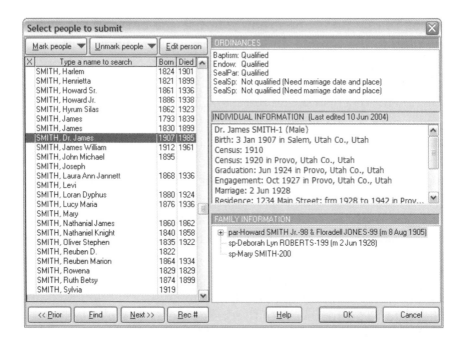

RootsMagic will display the selection screen where you can select the individuals you want to submit to TempleReady. This selection screen is the same as that described on page 181, except that it also shows which ordinances the highlighted person is qualified for. If the work is done, the completed date will be shown, and if the person is not qualified for the ordinance, RootsMagic will tell you the reason why.

Once you have marked the individuals to include, click OK and RootsMagic will bring up the File Save dialog where you can enter the name of the TempleReady file to create. Make sure you save the TempleReady file to your floppy drive rather than your hard disk. Click the Save button and RootsMagic will create the TempleReady file for you.

Take this floppy to your nearest Family History Center, run TempleReady and use this file as the input to TempleReady. TempleReady will process the names in the file, and will create a new disk which you can then take to the temple.

After TempleReady has read your file and created the disk to take to the temple, RootsMagic will let you automatically mark all the approved ordinances as "submitted". Simply click on the "Read submission file" button, insert the disk and select the file that TempleReady created, and RootsMagic will mark all approved ordinances as submitted (along with the current date). You are then ready to take the disk to the temple.

If you ever lose a temple disk after you have marked the ordinances as submitted, you can ask RootsMagic to remove "submitted" from the ordinances for a specific day. Click on the "Remove submitted" button on the TempleReady dialog, and RootsMagic will ask you for the date you reconciled your data. Enter the date, and RootsMagic will go through your database and remove the "submitted" status from all ordinances submitted on that date. You are then free to recreate a new TempleReady file for those individuals.

Updating Ordinance Information

RootsMagic provides an IGI search to help you easily find and update ordinance information. Make sure you are connected to the internet and do "Search, IGI search" to bring up the IGI search screen.

Starting an IGI Search Session

The first time you run the IGI Search, the browser window will take you to the login page for the FamilySearch website. If you have already registered on the FamilySearch website, enter your user name and password. If you haven't registered, you can register at this time.

> **✎ Note**
>
> Registering isn't a requirement to use the IGI Search feature, but it is necessary to register if you are LDS and want to be able to access the temple ordinance information.

If you have a user name and password and want RootsMagic to automatically log you in when you run the IGI Search, click the "Options" button on the IGI Search screen and enter your user name and password.

The IGI Search Screen

On the left side of the IGI Search screen is a list of every person in your RootsMagic database. The upper right side of the IGI Search screen displays information about the highlighted individual in your database. The lower right side of the IGI Search screen is a browser window to the FamilySearch IGI website.

As you move through the list on the left, the right side of the IGI Search screen will be updated to show the name, sex, facts, and family members of the highlighted person.

You can easily move to a person in the list by simply typing their name. As you type the name, the highlight bar will move to highlight the name closest to what you have typed.

Searching the IGI

There are two ways to search for a person in the IGI.

1. Highlight the person you want to search for and click the "Search IGI" button. RootsMagic will bring up a dialog box with options for searching the IGI. You can select the region to search, the type of event to search for, the date of that event, and a date range to choose how close the matches need to be. Select the options you want and click "OK" and RootsMagic will search the IGI and bring up a list of possible matches in the browser window.

2. Highlight the person you want to search for and click "QuickSearch" (or just double click on the person you want to search for). RootsMagic will analyze the data you have for the person and will perform a search for that person using the optimal search criteria for that person.

Search Options

Event to search by
- ○ All events
- ⦿ Birth / Christening
- ○ Marriage
- ○ Death / Burial

Event date to search for

Event year

`1959`

Year range

`Exact year` ▾

Region to search

Region

`North America` ▾

Country

`UNITED STATES` ▾

State/Province

`New Mexico` ▾

[OK] [Cancel]

After the list of possible matches is displayed, you can click one of the links to open the individual IGI record for the person. You can use the "Back" and "Forward" buttons just like you would in your regular internet browser.

Updating RootsMagic Records From the IGI

Any time you have an individual IGI record displayed on the IGI Search screen, you can click the "Update" button to compare the data you have for the person with the data the IGI has for the person. RootsMagic will display your RootsMagic record and the IGI record for the person side by side.

Checkboxes will appear for any birth, christening, death, burial, marriage, or LDS ordinance data in the IGI. You can mark any of the checkboxes and click the "Move selected data from IGI into RootsMagic" to copy the selected data from the IGI into your RootsMagic database. Leaving a box unchecked will cause RootsMagic to ignore that item from the IGI.

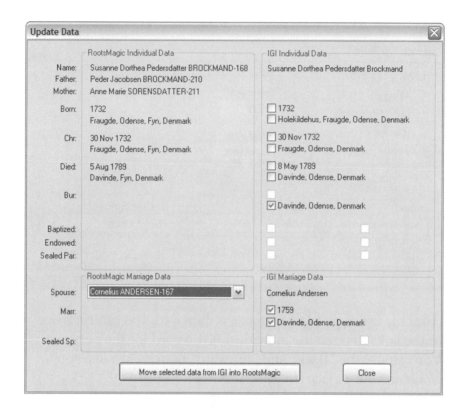

If you check an item and you already have information in your RootsMagic database, RootsMagic will create a new event with the new information and will not change the information you already have entered in your database.

If you need to edit information about a person (to clean up duplicate facts for example), you can highlight the person in the list and click the "Edit" button on the IGI Search screen to bring up the person's edit dialog.

Options

You can set various default options for the IGI search by clicking the Options button.

- **FamilySearch Login** – You can enter your FamilySearch user name and password so that RootsMagic will automatically log in for you when you run the IGI Search.

- **Default year range** – Lets you enter the date range that RootsMagic will use during QuickSearch, and will use as the default when doing a regular IGI Search.

- **Default region** – RootsMagic will try to determine the region to search in based on the information you already have entered for the person. If RootsMagic can't determine which region to search, it will use the region you select here as the default.

- **Always display last person searched for when doing IGI update** – By default, when you click the Update button it will normally show the person you last searched for even if you have moved the list highlight to someone else in the meantime. There may be cases where you want RM to let you update someone other than who you searched for. For example, you search for Mary Smith, and then update her. Her IGI page has a link to her husband who is also in your database. You click on the husband's link, but if you want to do an update you would normally have to do a search for him. If you uncheck that checkbox you can just highlight the husband in the list on the left and RM will let you update him without searching for him first.

RootsMagic Options

The more alternatives, the more difficult the choice. - Abbe'
D'Allanival

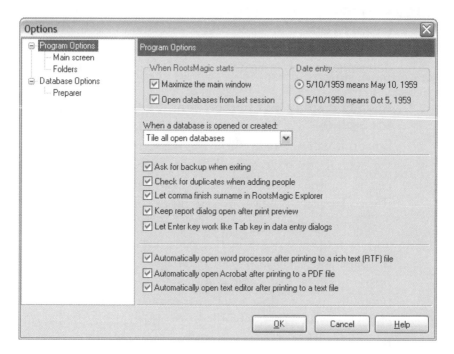

RootsMagic offers a number of options that you can use
to personalize the way the program and your databases
operate. To bring up the Options dialog, click the "Options"
button on the toolbar, or select "Tools, Options" from the main
menu. You can then choose which category of options you want
to change by clicking on an item on the left side of the Options
dialog.

Program Options

Program options are those options that affect the program as a
whole and are not specific to any one database. Select **"Program
options"** from the Options dialog list for the following choices.

Options

Program Options | Program Options
Main screen
Folders | When RootsMagic starts | Date entry
Database Options | ☑ Maximize the main window | ⦿ 5/10/1959 means May 10, 1959
Preparer | ☑ Open databases from last session | ◯ 5/10/1959 means Oct 5, 1959

When a database is opened or created:
Tile all open databases ▾

☑ Ask for backup when exiting
☑ Check for duplicates when adding people
☑ Let comma finish surname in RootsMagic Explorer
☑ Keep report dialog open after print preview
☑ Let Enter key work like Tab key in data entry dialogs

☑ Automatically open word processor after printing to a rich text (RTF) file
☑ Automatically open Acrobat after printing to a PDF file
☑ Automatically open text editor after printing to a text file

OK   Cancel   Help

When RootsMagic starts lets you tell RootsMagic whether to maximize the main window when the program starts, and whether to open up the databases that were open the last time you used the program.

Date entry determines whether RootsMagic interprets dates entered like 1/2/1997 as January 2, 1997 (US) or Febrary 1, 1997 (pretty much everywhere else).

When a database is opened or created tells RootsMagic whether to tile all windows, cascade all windows, or maximize the new window when opening or creating a database.

Ask for backup when exiting specifies whether RootsMagic will ask you if you want to make a backup when you exit the program.

Check for duplicates when adding people determines whether RootsMagic checks each time you add a new person to see if you may have already added them.

Let comma finish surnames in search screen enables or disables the feature in RootsMagic search screens where a comma can be typed to finish typing a surname during incremental searches.

Keep report dialog open after print preview tells RootsMagic to leave the report dialog on the screen when you close the print preview window. This lets you make changes to the report settings without having to reopen the report dialog.

Let Enter key work like Tab key in data entry dialogs makes the Enter key move from field to field instead of closing the dialog.

Automatically open word processor after printing to .RTF file tells RootsMagic whether to automatically open your word processor after it creates a Rich Text File printout. RootsMagic uses whatever word processor is "associated" with .rtf files in Windows.

Automatically open Acrobat after printing to PDF file tells RootsMagic whether to automatically open the Adobe Acrobat reader after it creates a PDF file. If you do not have the Acrobat reader installed on your system, you can download it for free from http://www.adobe.com.

Automatically open text editor after printing to text file tells RootsMagic whether to automatically open your text editor after it creates an ASCII text printout. RootsMagic uses whatever editor is "associated" with .txt files in Windows.

Main screen

RootsMagic allows you to change the font and colors used on the main screen with the "Main screen" item in the Options dialog.

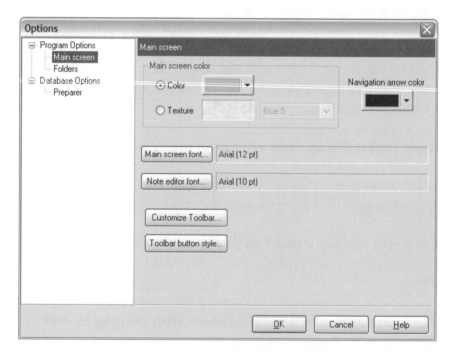

Main screen color lets you select the color for the main navigation views. You can select any color, or choose from several textures offered by RootsMagic. The textured backgrounds are only available if your Windows display settings are set to more than 256 colors. You can also select the color of the navigation arrows RootsMagic uses on the main screens.

Main screen font lets you select the font to be used on the main screen. RootsMagic will display the standard Windows font dialog, where you can select both the font typeface and size. If you select a font size that is too large to fit on the screen, RootsMagic will reduce the font size to fit.

Note editor font lets you select the font used on a person's note editing page. This allows you to choose a larger font while editing, but does not change the font used when printing the note (the font for printing notes is chosen from the reports dialog).

The "Customize Toolbar" button will let you add, rearrange or remove buttons on the toolbar. This is described in more detail on page 15.

The "Toolbar button style" button will let you select from several different styles of toolbar buttons, including large images, small images, small images with a text description, or the "classic" RootsMagic version 1 and 2 look.

Folders

The Folders option allows you to enter default folders where RootsMagic will look for certain types of files. You can just type in the full folder name, or click the button with the ellipses (…) to bring up a dialog to select the folder.

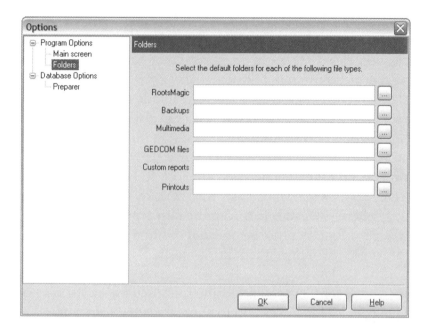

Database Options

Database options are those options that pertain to the current database.

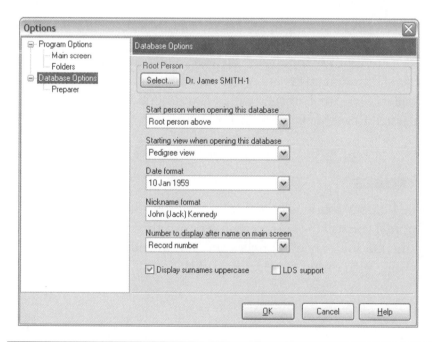

Root person lets you select the "root" person. The root person is the person that RootsMagic uses as the starting person on the main screen when you open a database. When you click "Select", RootsMagic will display the search screen, where you can select the new root person. **If you ever get lost in your database**, you can use the "Search, Go to root person" command to bring the root person back to the main screen.

Start person when opening this database lets you choose whether to start with the root person when opening the database, or whether to start with the person who was highlighted the last time you used the database.

Starting view when opening this database lets you specify whether RootsMagic will start up in the Pedigree, Family, or Descendants view.

Date format determines how RootsMagic will display dates you enter. You can actually enter dates in just about any format and RootsMagic will automatically convert them to the format you select here.

Nickname format determines how RootsMagic will display nicknames that you enter for people. You can have nicknames displayed with either "quotes" or (parentheses) around them.

Number to display after name on main screen lets you choose which number to display after the person's name in the info view on the main screen. You can choose between the record number (which RootsMagic assigns), the reference number (REFN, which you can add as a fact), or no number.

Display surnames uppercase lets you tell RootsMagic whether you want it to display and print surnames (last names) in all uppercase.

LDS support enables or disables the printing of LDS (Mormon) information on printouts. It also determines whether LDS information is displayed for the highlighted person on the main screen. If this box is checked, the letters B, E, P, and S may appear in the status area to the left of the name of the highlighted person, where B = baptism, E = endowment, P = sealing to parents, and S = sealing to spouse. These letters will also appear next to the name of every person on the pedigree, family, and descendant view that has LDS ordinance information entered.

Name of Preparer

The "Preparer" item in the options dialog allows you to enter the preparer (or submitter) name and address. This is the name and address that RootsMagic will print at the bottom of printouts if requested. Each database can have a different preparer.

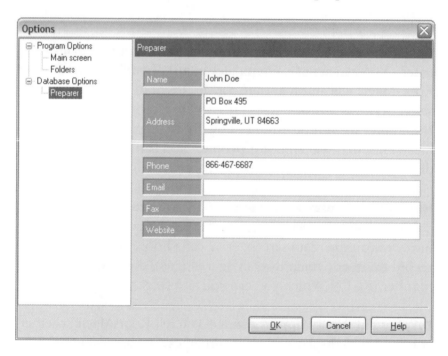

Quick Summary

Main Menu Commands

This section provides a brief description of each command in the
main menu. In addition, the page number is provided where the
feature is described in more detail.

❖ **File**
- ➢ **New** - Creates a new database (page 17)
- ➢ **Open** - Opens an existing database (page 19)
- ➢ **Search** – Search for RootsMagic or GEDCOM files on
  your computer (page 19)
- ➢ **Close** - Closes the currently selected database (page 20)
- ➢ **Rename** - Renames the current database (page 25)
- ➢ **Delete** - Deletes the current database from the hard drive
  (page 25)
- ➢ **Copy** – Creates a copy of the current database (page 25)
- ➢ **Print a report** - Brings up the Print Dialog where you can
  select and print a chart, form, book, etc. (page 97)
- ➢ **Printer setup** - Lets you select the printer and page
  orientation (portrait or landscape)
- ➢ **Import** - Imports GEDCOM, PAF, or Family Origins
  files into the current database (page 193)
- ➢ **Export GEDCOM** - Exports all or some of the data from
  the current database to a GEDCOM file (page 195)
- ➢ **TempleReady** – Creates and reconciles TempleReady
  files (page 250)
- ➢ **Backup** - Makes a back up copy of the current database
  (page 22)
- ➢ **Restore** - Restores a backed up database (page 25)
- ➢ **Rebuild indexes** – Rebuilds the database indexes, and
  optionally removes deleted records and reduces the size
  of the database in the process (page 25)
- ➢ **Properties** - Displays the number of records in the
  database (page 27)

➤ **Recent files** – Displays the most recent databases which you can select to open (page 19)
➤ **Exit** - Exits from RootsMagic
❖ **Edit**
➤ **Person** - Brings up the edit screen for the currently highlighted person (page 37)
➤ **Family** – Brings up the edit screen for the currently highlighted family (page 45)
➤ **Delete**
- **Person** - Removes the highlighted individual from the database (page 35)
- **Family** - Removes the highlighted family from the database (page 35)
➤ **Unlink**
- **from Spouse** - Unlinks the highlighted person from his/her currently displayed spouse (page 37)
- **from Parents** - Unlinks the highlighted person from his/her currently displayed parents (page 37)
➤ **Swap husband and wife** - Switches the husband and wife in a family (page 37)
➤ **Notes**
- **Person** - Brings up the note for the currently highlighted person (page 71)
- **Family** - Brings up the note for the currently highlighted family (page 71)
➤ **Sources**
- **Person** - Brings up the source dialog for the currently highlighted person (page 71)
- **Family** - Brings up the source dialog for the currently highlighted family (page 71)
➤ **Multimedia scrapbook**
- **Person** - Brings up the individual scrapbook for the currently highlighted person (page 89)
- **Family** - Brings up the family scrapbook for the currently highlighted family (page 89)
➤ **To Do**
- **Person** - Brings up the To Do List for the currently highlighted person (page 211)

- **Family** - Brings up the To Do List for the currently highlighted family (page 211)
- ➤ **Address**
  - **Person** - Brings up the current address for the currently highlighted person (page 43)
  - **Family** - Brings up the current address for the currently highlighted family (page 43)
- ➤ **LDS Ordinances** – Brings up the LDS ordinance template for the currently highlighted person (page 247)
- ❖ **Lists**
  - ➤ **Source list** - Brings up a list of all sources, and allows you to edit them (page 79)
  - ➤ **To-Do list** – Brings up a list of all todo tasks in your database and allows you to edit them (page 211)
  - ➤ **Address list** – Brings up a list of all addresses in your database and allows you to edit them (page)
  - ➤ **Repository list** - Brings up a list of all repositories, and allows you to edit them (page 87)
  - ➤ **Correspondence Log** – Brings up the correspondence log (page 215)
  - ➤ **Place list** - Brings up a list of all places in your database, and allows you to edit them (page 52)
  - ➤ **Fact type list** - Brings up a list of fact types, and allows you to add to or edit them (page 55)
- ❖ **Add**
  - ➤ **Individual** - Adds an unlinked individual to the database (page 28)
  - ➤ **Spouse** - Adds a spouse/partner to the highlighted person (page 28)
  - ➤ **Parents** - Adds parents to the highlighted person (page 28)
  - ➤ **Child** - Adds a child to the highlighted person (page 28)
- ❖ **View**
  - ➤ **Pedigree view** - Switches the main screen to the "Pedigree" view (page 10)
  - ➤ **Family view** - Switches the main screen to the "Family" view (page 11)

- ➢ **Descendants view** – Switches the main screen to the "Descendants" view (page 13)
- ➢ **View immediate family** - Displays all the immediate relatives of the highlighted person (page 64)
- ➢ **Toolbar** - Toggles the toolbar off and on (page 14)
- ➢ **Status Bar** - Toggles the status bar off and on (page 16)
- ❖ **Search**
  - ➢ **Person list** – Brings up the person list (RootsMagic Explorer) (page 60)
  - ➢ **Family list** – Brings up the family list (page 65)
  - ➢ **Go to root person** – Brings the "root" person back to the main screen (page 263)
  - ➢ **Search and replace** – Allows you to perform a search and replace in many fields of your database (page 233)
  - ➢ **Bookmarks** - Lets you mark the current person so you can quickly return to him or her (page 68)
  - ➢ **History** – Brings up a list of the most recently visited people in your database (page 68)
  - ➢ **Back** – Moves to the most recently visited person on the main screen (page 68)
  - ➢ **Forward** – Moves forward to the most recently visited person on the main screen (page 68)
  - ➢ **Internet search** – Looks up a person from your database on the internet (page 70)
  - ➢ **IGI search** – Searches the FamilySearch IGI site and lets you update ordinance information (page 253)
- ❖ **Reports**
  - ➢ **Publisher** – Print a book made up of multiple report types (page 185)
  - ➢ **Pedigree chart** - Prints a pedigree chart for the highlighted person (page 104)
  - ➢ **Family group sheet** - Prints a family group sheet for the highlighted family (page 107)
  - ➢ **Narrative reports** - Prints a book starting with the highlighted person (page 113)
  - ➢ **Charts**

- **Wall charts** – Prints large ancestor, descendant, and hourglass wall charts (page 158)
- **Timeline charts** – Prints graphical timelines with bars representing the life span of people (page 158)
- **Box charts** – Prints ancestor and descendant box charts which can be included in printed reports (page 117)
- **Relationship Chart** - Prints a box chart that shows you exactly how the two people are related (page 152)
- **Photo tree** - Prints a photo pedigree ancestor tree (page 155)
- **Blank wallcharts** – Opens up RootsMagic Chart so that you can load and edit existing wallcharts that you have created and saved (page 158)
- ➢ **Individual summary** - Prints a summary for the highlighted person (page 151)
- ➢ **Lists** - Lets you select a list type and print it (page 121)
- ➢ **Calendar** - Prints a calendar with birthdays and / or anniversaries (page 149)
- ➢ **Custom reports** - Lets you design and print a custom report (page 174)
- ➢ **Scrapbooks** – Prints a scrapbook for a person, family, source or place (page 154)
- ➢ **Blank forms** - Prints a blank form (page 156)
- ➢ **PrintMyChart.com** – Takes you to an online discount wall chart printing service (page 173)
- ❖ **Tools**
  - ➢ **Merge records**
    - **Duplicate search / merge** – Finds potential duplicate records and allows you to merge them if desired (page 201)
    - **Automatic merges** - Automatically merges as many duplicate records as it can (page 206)
    - **Manual merge** - Merges two duplicate records together (page 201)

- **View "not duplicates" list** – Opens the list of records which you have marked as not duplicates (page 201)
- **Problem Search**
  - **Problem list** – Creates a list of potential problems in your database (page 222)
  - **View "not a problem" list** – Displays a list of items you have marked as "not a problem" (page 222)
- **Count trees in database** – Counts the total number of distinct trees in your database (page 234)
- **Spell check** – Spell checks the notes in your database (page 230)
- **Set living** – Lets you set or clear the Living flag for any group of people (page 225)
- **Color code people** – Lets you set a color on the main screen for any group of people (page 226)
- **Set relationships** – Sets the relationship of everyone in the database to the current person (page 225)
- **Relationship calculator** - Calculates the relationship between any two people (page 229)
- **Soundex calculator** - Calculates the Soundex code for a surname (page 230)
- **Date calculator** - Allows you to do date calculations (page 227)
- **GenSmarts suggestions** – Runs GenSmarts (if installed) to provide research suggestions for current person (page 214)
- **Create a Shareable CD** – Lets you create and burn a CD of your data to share with others (page 190)
- **Options**- Lets you change the program and database settings (page 258)
- ❖ **Internet**
  - **Create a website** - Creates a website (HTML) from the information in your database, and allows you to upload it to your home page (page 236)
  - **RootsMagic.com** – Opens the browser to RootsMagic.com

- ➢ **Message Boards** - Internet message boards
- ➢ **FAQ** – Opens the browser to the RootsMagic Frequently Asked Questions page
- ➢ **Technical support** – Opens the browser to the RootsMagic technical support page
- ➢ **Family reunion planner** - Hundreds of ideas, tips, and resources for planning the perfect family reunion (requires Internet access)
- ❖ **Window**
  - ➢ **Tile** - Arranges your open databases side by side
  - ➢ **Cascade** - Arranges your open databases in a cascading arrangement
  - ➢ **Arrange icons** - Arranges any open databases that you have minimized
  - ➢ **Close all** - Closes all currently open databases
- ❖ **Help**
  - ➢ **Help topics** - Brings up the RootsMagic help system
  - ➢ **Tip of the Day** – Opens the Tip of the Day dialog
  - ➢ **Check for updates** – Opens the browser to check if there are any updates to the version of RootsMagic you are using.
  - ➢ **Technical support** – Opens the browser to the RootsMagic technical support page
  - ➢ **FAQ** – Opens the browser to the RootsMagic Frequently Asked Questions page

Built-in Fact Types

Fact Type	Description
Adoption	Pertaining to creation of a child-parent relationship that does not exist biologically.
Also known as	Another name by which a person is known by.
Ancestral file number	A unique permanent record file number of an individual record stored in Ancestral File.
Annulment	Declaring a marriage void from the beginning (never existed).
Baptism	The event of baptism (not LDS), performed in infancy or later.
Baptism (LDS)	The event of baptism performed at age eight or later by priesthood authority of the LDS Church.
Bar Mitzvah	The ceremonial event held when a Jewish boy reaches age 13.
Bas Mitzvah	The ceremonial event held when a Jewish girl reaches age 13, also known as "Bat Mitzvah."
Birth	The event of entering into life.
Blessing	A religious event of bestowing divine care or intercession. Sometimes given in connection with a naming ceremony.
Burial	The event of the proper disposing of the mortal remains of a deceased person.
Census	The event of the periodic count of the population for a designated locality, such as a national or state Census.
Christening	The religious event (not LDS) of baptizing and/or naming a child.
Christening (adult)	The religious event (not LDS) of baptizing and/or naming an adult person.
Confirmation	The religious event (not LDS) of conferring the gift of the Holy Ghost and, among Protestants, full church membership.
Cremation	Disposal of the remains of a person's body by fire.
Death	The event when mortal life terminates.
Degree	A degree earned by a person (see also Graduation).
Description	The physical characteristics of a person, place, or thing.
Divorce	An event of dissolving a marriage through civil action.
Divorce filed	An event of filing for a divorce by a spouse.
Education	Indicator of a level of education attained.
Election	An event where a person is elected to some office.
Emigration	An event of leaving one's homeland with the intent of residing elsewhere.
Endowment (LDS)	A religious event where an endowment ordinance for an individual was performed by priesthood authority in an LDS temple.
Engagement	An event of recording or announcing an agreement between two people to become married.
Excommunication	An event where a person is expelled from the communion of a church and deprived of its rights, privileges, and advantages.
First Communion	A religious rite, the first act of sharing in the Lord's supper as part of church worship.
Graduation	An event of awarding educational diplomas or degrees to individuals.

Illness	The state or condition of being sick.
Immigration	An event of entering into a new locality with the intent of residing there.
Living	The state of being alive at a particular time.
Marriage	A legal, common-law, or customary event of creating a family unit of a man and a woman as husband and wife.
Marriage Bann	An event of an official public notice given that two people intend to marry.
Marriage contract	An event of recording a formal agreement of marriage, including the prenuptial agreement in which marriage partners reach agreement about the property rights of one or both, securing property to their children.
Marriage license	An event of obtaining a legal license to marry.
Marriage settlement	An event of creating an agreement between two people contemplating marriage, at which time they agree to release or modify property rights that would otherwise arise from the marriage.
Military	The state of being in the military service, whether during peacetime or war.
Miscellaneous	An event which is so general that it doesn't fit in any category.
Mission	The state of being sent to an area to spread religion or carry on educational or charitable activities.
Namesake	An individual who a person is named after.
Nationality	The national heritage of an individual.
Naturalization	The event of obtaining citizenship.
Occupation	The type of work or profession of an individual.
Ordination	A religious event of receiving authority to act in religious matters.
Probate	An event of judicial determination of the validity of a will. May indicate several related court activities over several dates.
Property	Pertaining to possessions such as real estate or other property of interest.
Reference number	A description or number used to identify an item for filing, storage, or other reference purposes.
Religion	A religious denomination to which a person is affiliated or for which a record applies.
Residence	The act of dwelling at an address for a period of time.
Retirement	An event of exiting an occupational relationship with an employer after a qualifying time period.
Sealing to parents (LDS)	A religious event pertaining to the sealing of a child to his or her parents in an LDS temple ceremony.
Sealing to spouse (LDS)	A religious event pertaining to the sealing of a husband and wife in an LDS temple ceremony.
Separation	An event where the conjugal cohabitation of a husband and wife ceases.
Social security number	A number assigned by the United States Social Security Administration. Used for tax identification purposes.
Stillborn	The event where an infant is dead at birth.
Will	A legal document treated as an event, by which a person disposes of his or her estate, to take effect after death. The event date is the date the will was signed while the person was alive.